HISTORY OF UPPER ASSAM, UPPER BURMAH AND NORTH EASTERN FRONTIER

HISTORY OF UPPER ASSAM, UPPER BURMAH AND NORTH EASTERN FRONTIER

By

LESLIE WATERFIELD SHAKESPEAR

GYAN

ISBN : 978-81-212-1695-1(PB)

First Published, 1914

Published, 2018

Published by

GYAN

Gyan Publishing House
5, Ansari Road
Daryaganj, New Delhi-110002
Phone: 011-47034999, 9811692060
www.gyanbooks.com
E-mail: books@gyanbooks.com

Printed at: G. Print Process, Delhi.

TO THE ASSAM MILITARY POLICE FORCE

With which I had the honour of serving several happy interesting years—the Wardens of our long stretch of North-Eastern Marches; who, since we were brought into touch with this far-off corner of our Indian possessions have borne the heat, burden, and stress of every expedition (officially recognised or otherwise) with a cheerful willingness and zeal which has won the approbation of all who have worked with them, but whose labours too frequently pass unnoticed—I dedicate this humble work.

"Floreant custodes terminorum Imperii nostri."

L. W. SHAKESPEAR
(Colonel, 2nd Goorkhas).

DEHRA DOON, 1912-13.

PREFACE

As I have found no book dealing completely and succinctly with Assam, its border land now so much in the public eye, and the many wild and interesting peoples dwelling along that border, which obliges the student to search through many books before arriving at the points of interest desired (if even then they are obtained), I have endeavoured to collect materials from all—to me—possible sources, and weaving them into narrative form, to produce something useful and readable at least for those who care about that little-known but very interesting corner of India. The success of my article which the *Army Review* printed in October, 1912, on this subject, has led me to attempt something more complete in detail; and with all its shortcomings I trust it may be appreciated by those interested in the past and future of this fertile and lovely land. If any criticisms may seem too trenchant, I trust the hope that there are those who will in the future benefit by statements of facts may be recognised as a sufficient excuse for having ventured into such, possibly to some, undesirable spheres. In this connection a remark of Commander Bellairs, R.N., in his interesting article on "Secrecy and Discussion," which ran to the effect that, if there is no criticism, which naturally goes with discussion, the teachings of history are apt to be perverted—may still further strengthen my excuse. Without certain of the books mentioned in the Bibliography this could not have been attempted, and I desire to record my high appreciation of, and indebtedness to, the particular labours of their authors; and my gratitude to the Librarian of the Imperial Library, Calcutta, for his personal assistance so courteously given. My thanks are also due to certain friends who have helped with photographs, namely, those of the Ābors, Mishmis, and some of the photos dealing with Marām monoliths and Nagas where I was unable to go personally; the rest of the photos and sketches are my own.

I may add that this book has been *viséd* by Army Headquarters, whose suggested alterations, omissions, have been duly attended to.

L. W. SHAKESPEAR
(Colonel, 2nd Goorkhas).

CONTENTS

CHAPTER I

CHAPTER II

CHAPTER III

CHAPTER IV

CHAPTER V

LIST OF ILLUSTRATIONS

MAPS AND PLATES

BIBLIOGRAPHY

K. S. Macdonald's "Kāmrup and Gauhati in Assam," 1902.

C. C. Lowis's "Tribes of Burma," 1910.

Hamilton and Syme's "Account of Burman Empire and Kingdom of Assam," 1839.

Gaits' "History of Assam," 1906.

W. W. Hunter's "The Indian Empire," 1886. "Sketch of the Singphos and Inland Trade of the Irrawadi and their Connection with N.E. Assam." 1847.

J. T. Moore's "Twenty Years in Assam," 1901.

T. Kinney's "Old Times in Assam," 1896.

S. O. Bishop's "Sketches in Assam," 1885.

T. T. Cooper's "The Mishmi Hills," 1873.

Bastian's "Völkersstämme am Brahmaputra."

"The Upper Burma Gazetteer," Volume I, Part 1.

Prince H. d'Orléan's "Tonkin to India," 1898.

T. T. Cooper's "Travels of a Pioneer of Commerce," 1871.

"Frontier and Overseas Expeditions from India," 1907.

General Sir J. Johnston's "My Experiences in Manipur and the Naga Hills," 1896.

Ferishta's "History of the Moghul Empire."

Colonel J. Johnston's "Captain Welsh's Expedition to Assam, 1792–94." 1912.

Mackenzie's "History of Assam and the N.E. Tribes," 1883.

Hosie's "Journey in 1883 through Ssu-chuan and Yünnan."

Bryan Hodgson's "Kocch, Bodo, and Dimal Tribes," 1847.

The Reverend Endel's "History of the Kachāris."

Major Hannay's "Pamphlet in the J. A. S. Bengal on the Ruins East of Sadiya," 1848.

Errol Gray's "Diary of a Journey to the Bor Hkamti Country," 1893.

B. G. Carey's "Chin Hills Gazetteer," 1896.

HISTORY OF UPPER ASSAM, UPPER BURMAH AND NORTH-EASTERN FRONTIER

CHAPTER I

In spite of the interest Assam has furnished to ethnologists in the past, due to the numerous and curious peoples living in and round it, as well as from the more recent military expeditions and the awakening of China with her ambition to monopolise the country lying to the north and east of its practically unknown borders; there is hardly any part of India which is less known to the general public. It has indeed probably only been heard of by the public as a tea-producing district, and one which has, since Lord Curzon's famous "Partition," become connected with the sedition of Eastern Bengal which lies immediately south of Assam proper. It is not thought of as ever having possessed a stirring history or an old civilisation; though this latter is attested by the numerous ancient forts, temples, and certain old high roads such as the Kāmāli Alli running 350 miles from Cooch Behar to Narainpur, still in use in parts, which are to be found scattered up and down the length and breadth of the land. These probably only reveal a small portion of what may still remain for the archæologist when the jungle and forest which still cover so great a portion of Assam may be removed, as settlers and their cultivation gradually extend. That it was a densely populated country in the far-off past is shown by the extensive ruins of Kamātāpur near Cooch Behar in the west, stated by Buchanan Hamilton to be upwards of nineteen miles round and flourishing up to the end of the fifteenth century, when it fell a prey to the Moghuls—by the extensive ruins of old fortifications in the neighbourhood of Baliapāra not far from the foot of the Aka Hills—by the famous temples of Kāmakhya near Gauhati, and those at Charaideo, near which latter are also the remains of the old capital of Garhgaon. In the extreme eastern corner of Assam, viz., in the angle formed by the rivers Dibong and Dikrang within fifteen miles of our present frontier post of Sadiya and no great distance from the point whence General Bower's recent Abor expedition made its start, lie the extensive ruins of Bishmaknagar (Kundina) and a large fort of hewn stone together with four or five excavated tanks.

This showing that what is now almost a "terra incognita" to us, covered with more or less impenetrable jungle, was once the centre of a thriving community.

Mr. Kinney, who knew the Dibrughar district well, alludes to the former high state of cultivation and energy of a people now sunk in apathy and opium eating, as evinced by ruins of magnificent buildings and raised roadways found all over the country. The fine old Tengrai Raj Alli connecting Rangpur with Nāmrup for instance, is frequently met with in the heart of the forest, and parts of it in the more open spaces are in use still. Mr. T. T. Cooper also writing in 1873 of eastern Assam again testifies to the energy and civilisation formerly characteristic of this people and forming a striking contrast to the lethargic existence of the present-day scanty population. He says: "The contemplation of these ruins surrounded by almost impenetrable jungle which has overgrown the once fertile and well cultivated fields of a people that has almost passed away, is calculated to strike one with an intense desire to learn more of the history of those terrible events which robbed a fertile land of a vast and industrious population, converting it into a wilderness of swamps and forests."

Again the extensive region of the dense Nambhor Forest lying between Lumding Junction (on the Assam and Bengal Railway) and Golaghat and bordered by the Mikir and Naga Hills is known to cover ground at one time owned by the strong Kachāri clans in a high state of civilisation with their capital at Dimāpur on the Dhansiri river almost in the centre of the forest. When the engineers, Messrs. Thornhill, Buckle, and Venters in 1896–97 were arranging the earthwork of the Assam and Bengal Railway north from Lumding, they came on causeways, canals, and sites of buildings, notably in the vicinity of Rangapahar and Dimāpur now covered with jungle; which jungle, however, forest experts speak of as being of no greater age than 200 years. As we shall see later on, history shows us the Kachāris were overwhelmed by the Ahoms and had their capital sacked in the middle of the sixteenth century, which was then deserted together with the entire region, and this was never re-occupied by either nation.

Just these few facts go to prove that Assam, spoken of in old Moghul writings as " a land of mystery and witchcraft," does possess an interest which will repay those who care to peruse the illuminating works on this country by Messrs. Blochmann, Gait, Prinsep, and others. When these are read and one realises to what an extent civilisation had reached, the large armies that operated up and down the Brahmaputra valley, the depth of its religions, the engineering and architectural work left behind, one is inclined to wonder what has become of it all and of the peoples ; and what caused the decay of power which permitted its once thriving valleys to be now choked and buried in densest forests ? For the people now met with in Assam are a peaceful, almost effeminate race, in no great numbers, addicted in a large measure to opium eating, and not disposed to diligent labour ; whence the necessity for importing the great numbers of coolies from India required to work on the tea gardens.

It is generally assumed that climatic conditions tended very largely to bring about this state of decay, at all events where the people were concerned ; for the climate is a distinctly enervating one, and each race that has settled there has, in course of time, lost its vigour and been supplanted by hardier folk, who in their turn have, in spite of material progress as to civilisation, succumbed to the love of ease and luxury born of an enervating climate in a highly fertile land.

As to vanished cities, forts and other landmarks of

the past, their disappearance is attributable to the soft alluvial soils of the valleys, which permit the easy task for rivers of cutting for themselves fresh channels, and so frequently destroying and carrying away the towns and buildings which history tells us did exist along their banks. Examples of this are to be found in comparing a map of 1790 with one of about 1860 when the Brahmaputra's course below Gauhati will be seen to have shifted close on fifty miles within this

BRAHMAPUTRA AND RIVER STEAMER AT GAUHATI.

period; while some twenty miles from the right bank of the same river between Nalbāri and Hājo are to be seen the arches of an ancient bridge once spanning an old course of the river, and known as the "Sil Sako." It stands now in the centre of a lake surrounded by miles of forest, and had several of its arches destroyed by the great earthquake of 1897. In the far eastern corner of the province beyond and not far from Sadiya are signs that the Brahmaputra and Lohit rivers flowed in the far-off past much closer to the foot of the Ābor and Mishmi hills, and Hannay states his opinion that it was the gradual changing of the river's course further and further south which led to the abandonment of the cities of Kundina (Bishmaknagar) and Prithiminagar. Added to this force of Nature come those of earthquakes by which Assam has suffered seriously, and the marvellously rapid growth of vegetation; which when unchecked in a few years spreads, chokes up valleys, and obliterates, as in the case of the Dhansiri and Kopili valleys, all traces of former towns and buildings. Although this volume is intended to deal chiefly with tribes dwelling along the whole of our north-eastern borderland it will not be without interest to trace the history of the country from the most ancient times as revealed by rock-cut inscriptions and legends, the first contact of the Moghuls with the Ahoms then the ruling race here, and finally the appearance of the English on the scene.

The particular part of Assam this history deals with, viz., upper Assam from Goalpāra to Sadiya, comprises the whole valley of the Brahmaputra with a length of nearly 450 miles and a varying breadth of sixty to eighty miles, covering an area of over 30,000 square miles. To the north and east high mountains shut it off from Thibet and Bhutān, on the west it joins Bengal, while south and east another mountainous region—that of the Patkoi and Barail ranges—separates it from Burma and south-western China. It is thus almost completely surrounded by mountains which are inhabited by more or less savage tribes. The early history of Assam being purely legendary it is practically impossible to lift the veil lying over it, though here and there a little light comes in from ancient inscriptions in India, such, for instance, as that on the famous Allahabad pillar erected in Chandragupta's time, 316–292 B.C., whereon we learn that Kāmarupa (as Assam was called in early days) was known of then as a State lying away east of Nepal to which King Chandragupta's fame had penetrated; and it had then, probably under its Hindoo Khettri Kings (the very earliest rulers in Assam), attained to a degree of civilisation almost equal to that of the Hindu dynasties in India of those days.

A copper-plate inscription records an invasion by Vikramaditya, King of Ujjain, about 57 B.C., and as he was a Buddhist it is probable he fostered that religion in the land where, as we shall see, it never took a serious hold. Major Hannay of the old Assam Light Infantry, who made considerable research into the ancient history of Assam, is of opinion that Kāmarupa was one of the earliest conquests of the Hindu Khettri Kings about 400 B.C., and was the seat of that primitive form of Hinduism which existed previous to Buddhism, and which again was followed in the middle of the fifteenth century by Brahminical Hinduism introduced by certain Brahmins from the city of Gaur, in Bengal.

Another inscription shows a Gupta King, by name Samūdra, at the end of the fourth century A.D. exacting tribute from Kāmarupa, and from the following century this country came under the Gupta dynasty, lasting up to the first half of the ninth century. A Rajput, called Itari, rising to power, started the Pal dynasty, taking the name of Dharm Pal. Twelve kings of this dynasty are said to have reigned between

830 and 1140 A.D., and these in their turn gave way to that of the Senas, who however, being of Bengal, ruled only the western part of Kāmarupa.

That Assam and the Hukong Valley to the Irrawadi river and beyond, formed as it were a natural highway for old-time Indian kings with a desire for conquests far afield is known, and Forlong, in his researches, states an Indian King named Samudra (not the one previously mentioned) was ruling in upper Burma about 105 A.D., and that they were Hindus from that locality who led the Shans far down the Mekhong river into Siam; while earlier still Chinese chronicles state an Indian prince from Cambōd in north-west India was reigning in Cambōdia, giving the name of his original homeland to his new territory. These chronicles also say adventurers from India founded kingdoms in Java and Malaya as far back as 166 A.D., and also that merchants from Alexandria or some other Roman port visited China a little later, travelling viâ Chiampa, the old name for Siam. All these Indians with their armies must have got there via Assam and the low passes of the Patkoi Range into the Hukong Valley and so further east. The difficult mountainous regions stretching from the Patkoi away down south to Arrakan precluded the possibility of passing masses of men through them, while long sea voyages were unknown to the Indian peoples of those days. Though certain historians are of opinion that Hindus from the ancient sea coast kingdom of Kalinga (Madras side) did make voyages to Java and that the Hindu ruined cities and temples found there are their handiwork.

Other copper plate inscriptions found in Assam show various lands having been made over to Brahmin priests by certain rulers of the Pal dynasty between 990 and 1142 A.D., whose names are thus arrived at; otherwise the first authentic information we have of Kāmarupa, viz., the country lying between the Karatoya river (flowing past Julpigori into the Brahmaputra near Goalundo) and Sadiya, is by the hand of the great Chinese traveller, Huien Tsiang, who came

ANCIENT TEMPLES IN UPPER ASSAM.

to this country in 630 A.D., visiting Gauhati and other places of sanctity.

Of the three strong tribes who long held dominion in different parts of upper Assam, the earliest to arrive in the country is surmised to have been the Kachāris, whose original habitat is believed to have been along the foot of the Darjiling hills and the Morang tract, which was known to the Nepalese as the "Kaccha country." These then travelled east and crossed the Brahmaputra, settling in what is now the Nowgong district between Jorhat and Gauhati.

Spreading from there, they populated the Dhansiri and Kopili valleys and all eastern Assam, eventually crossing the southern hills and occupying the present district of Cachar, to which they gave the name of their ancient home, after they had ousted the Tippera people.

The Chutiyas, an offshoot of the Kachāri tribe, alone used a written character, but made no use of it in recording events.

The second tribe to rise into prominence were the Kocches, allies to the Kachāris, whose home lay just east of the Karatoya river where the little State of Cooch Behar is now. Their kingdom when consolidated comprised the whole of Kāmarupa, which then lay chiefly on the north bank of the Brahmaputra, with Gauhati and the country towards Goalpāra on the south bank.

As these two tribes had kept no records, our information regarding them up to the arrival on the scene of the Ahoms, comes from Mahomedan historians who recorded the different Moghul invasions, and from local legends, here and there substantiated by rock-cut and copper plate inscriptions which have come to light at Tezpur, Gauhati and elsewhere.

The third and the most important tribe are the Ahoms, because they possessed a literature of a sort and certainly kept written historical records—" buranjis " as they are called, meaning " stores of instruction for the ignorant," whereby we have a definite history of events in upper Assam since their arrival there about 1220 A.D. They were non-Buddhist Shans of the great Tai race who inhabited the old kingdom of Pông (the Mogoung of the present day) which stretched from the upper Chindwyn to the upper

Irrawadi rivers; and these people held sway in the Brahmaputra valley until the troubles with the Burmese in 1825 led to the appearance on the scene of the last dominant Power—the English. Besides these three large tribes, other smaller ones ruled in outlying portions of the country, as, for instance, the Chutiyas, owning the country between the Subansiri and Disang rivers, and the Morans who dwelt opposite the Chutiyas on the south bank of the Brahmaputra, east of the present Sibsagor. Both are of the same stock as the Kachāris, but the former is of very ancient origin, the Deori Chutiyas claiming proudly to belong to the descendants of the Hindu Khettri line, which Hannay says seems to be corroborated by the fact that the Chutiya language, now only known to the Deoris or temple priests, contains a large proportion of Sanscrit and Hindu words plus a certain amount of Burmese from the Shan conquerors, whose "buranjis" state the Chutiyas were the only possessors of a written language they met with at the time of their advent into Assam. Whether the Chutiyas were the original builders of the cities of Bishmaknagar (Kundina) and Prithiminagar beyond Sadiya, and now covered by forests, is not known, but Hannay is of opinion that they were occupied in the time of the Khettri Kings over 2,000 years ago.

CHAPTER II

We will now turn to a historical review of the three great tribes, beginning with the Kachāris, who, as we have seen before, trekked in past ages from the "Khaccha country," which lay roughly between the Brahmaputra and the Kusi rivers along the foot of the Himalayas into the country beyond the Brahmaputra, settling first in what is now the Nowgong district, and after long ages extending their dominions up the great valley to about where Sadiya now stands, and southwards up the Kopili valley and later still up the Dhansiri and Doyang valleys to where they emerge from the hills. Bryan Hodgson (1847) is one of the authorities for this statement as to the original home of the Kachāris and Kocches, both being at least linguistically allied; though Endle, in an excellent work on the Kachāris, places their ancestral home in Thibet and China, and concludes that they migrated in two streams into the rich Brahmaputra valley—one stream entering western Assam through the valleys of the Tista, Dharla, and Sankōsh rivers, and founding the kingdom of Kāmarupa; while the other stream found its way down the Subansiri, Dihong, and Dibang valleys into eastern Assam. He classes the Chutiyas, who long held sway round about

Sadiya, as being a clan of the great Kachāri nation left behind as the tide of migration rolled west and south. Both he and Hodgson hold that in very early days they were the dominant races in Assam; but the latter goes further and states they are the aborigines of Assam; in fact he classes them with the Tamulian aboriginal inhabitants of India such as Gonds, Bhils, etc., and does so through their peculiar physical capability of being able to live healthily in forest and swampy localities where no other human beings can exist. He therefore concludes that this capability could only have been evolved after a lapse of a very great space of time, which he computes at thirty centuries, so we may as well assume that the Kachāris and Kocches are of the aboriginal races in India. They appear to have been a peaceful and flourishing race, given to agriculture, and seem to have lived in amity with the rising Kocch nation on the far side of the Brahmaputra, with the exception of trouble in 1562, when they were defeated by the Kocch king Nar Narain; while they also traded with Dacca and Bengal viâ Goalpāra. It was evidently from Bengal that they got their ideas of building with bricks, for in those far-off days neither of the other nations built permanent towns or forts, their defences being entirely of the nature of earthworks, and their buildings of wood and bamboo. A few ancient temples only in upper Assam were then built of masonry, whereas the remains at Dimāpur, for instance, which flourished centuries before the Ahoms arrived, show us the Kachāris knew all about the art of brick making and permanent buildings; while the style in which they worked points to having been copied from Bengal, the nearest civilised country to them. To anyone nowadays travelling by rail from Haflong to near Golaghat, or from Golaghat by road to Nichuguard at the foot of the Naga hills, it is difficult to realise that this densely forested region covers the sites of many old cities and vast areas of cultivation, the names of which, such as Maihām, Jāmaguri, Dijoa, alone remain in old Ahom accounts. Of the three valleys mentioned before, the Kopili is the only one which has not lapsed into such complete desolation; for the reason that the Kachāris were able to hold on to this tract much longer, almost up to the beginning of the nineteenth century; whereas the other two, viz., the Dhansiri and Doyang valleys, ceased to belong to them some 300 years earlier. By the time the Ahoms were making themselves felt as a power in the region round Sadiya and Nāmrup, the Kachāri people held the country up to the Dikkoo river flowing past Sibsagor, and here they came into contact with the Ahoms about the beginning of the fourteenth century. Constant friction occurring, and the Ahoms being strengthened by a fresh influx of emigrants from the east, the Kachāris gradually withdrew until in the end of the fifteenth century they took up arms with intent to recover lost lands so successfully, that in 1490 they badly defeated the Ahoms at Dampuk on the Dikkoo river, which they once more made their boundary. Thirty years later commenced the long series of wars in which the Ahoms, having reduced their other enemies, the Chutiyas and Morans, and also to a certain extent the Kooches, had time to turn with all their strength against the Kachāri peoples; for in the early part of the sixteenth century they were pressed back until they lost all territory east of Golaghat, the Ahoms building a strong earthwork fort at Marangi, a little south of Jorhat, by which to hold what they had taken. Before a year was over a Kachāri effort against Marangi led to the Ahoms ascending the Dhansiri and Doyang valleys in two strong armies where, after successful actions at Bardua and Maihām, the Ahoms

LAST REMAINING GATEWAY TO THE OLD KACHĀRI FORT AT DIMĀPUR.

retired. The sites of these places are no longer known. Five years later, the Kachāris, still smarting under these defeats, attacked the Ahoms in the neighbourhood of Golaghat, and this time the latter took a large force victoriously up the Dhansiri as far as the Kachāri capital of Dimāpur, where, after a stiff action, in which the Kachāri king was killed and his head sent to Charaideo, the Ahoms dictated terms and, setting up one Detsing as king, they retired out of the country. Five years later, however, Detsing quarrelled with the Ahom king Sūkmūngūng, who, with a large army, advanced first up both sides of the Doyang, where the Kachāris made but slight resistance, and then moved into and up the Dhansiri to the capital.

Here the Kachāris after a desperate defence were completely defeated and the city sacked. The Ahoms now took over this entire tract of country, but as they never occupied it and the former Kachāri occupants had either been killed or had retired to found the new capital at Maibong in what is now the North Cachar hills, the Dhansiri and Doyang valleys soon relapsed into jungle, which in later times became known as the Nambhor forest. Ahom "buranjis" record that in 1637 the route for communication between Ahoms and Kachāris was viâ Koliabar, Nowgong, and the Kopili valley; as the Dhansiri valley route was impossible and the country depopulated, Maibong, now a small station on the Assam-Bengal Railway, lies a few miles north of the civil station of Haflong, and by the end of the sixteenth century had become a town of considerable size and strength according to old accounts, and from what remains for us to judge by, namely traces of what were strong walls, gateways, temples, etc. One curious rock-cut temple has a record cut into the stone showing the sacred edifice to have been made about 1721 in the reign of Chandra Narain. In the beginning of the seventeenth century the Kachāris were still in possession of the north of Nowgong district, where it borders the Brahmaputra valley, and to the south of the same along the Jamūna and Kopili valleys where stood the once flourishing towns of Rāhā, Doboka, Demera; and they had also long since been the dominant power in the Cachar plains (Surma valley), where they had driven back the original occupants, the Tippera people. They now tried their strength against the adjoining strong hill tribe, the Jaintias, whose Raja was defeated and his capital, Khāspur, taken. A few years later, namely in 1606, trouble again occurred with the Ahoms and the two forces met at Dharmtika, where the Ahom king, Pratap Sing, was successful, but later received a signal defeat at Rāhā near Nowgong; after which he withdrew his forces owing to fears of an approaching Mahomedan invasion. A more or less peaceful period then set in for the Kachāris lasting some ninety years, when in 1696 Rudra Sing, one of the greatest of the Ahom monarchs, made war upon the Kachāri king, Tamradhoj, who had proclaimed his independence, and sent an army of 37,000 up the Dhansiri to Dijoa, and another of 34,000 viâ Rāhā and the Kopili valley. The objective of each was Maibong, the capital, and both forces had to make their own roads through the forest as they advanced. The former force having defeated the Kachāris at Dijoa (now Mohan Dijoa on the north-eastern edge of the Mikir hills), reached Maibong first, and in a pitched battle crushed Tamradhoj's forces and captured the city, demolishing its walls and defences. The Rāhā army having had enormous difficulties to contend with in cutting its way through dense forests arrived late, but was used to continue the war into Cachar, having Khāspur city as its objective. Much sickness in his army, and finding great difficulty in the màtter of food supplies, caused Rudra Sing to give up the attempt and withdraw his troops. The Jaintias never having got over their defeat by the Kachāris, began trouble in 1705, and after a series of small actions their Raja managed by treachery to seize the person of Tamradhoj, who appealed for aid to his old enemy the Ahom Rudra Sing. This was replied to by the sending of two Ahom columns through the Jaintia country in 1707, one of which got through the hills, defeated the Jaintia forces, and occupied the city of Jaintiapur on the south side of those hills. Both the Raja of Jaintia and his prisoner Tamradhoj were taken, sent to Bishnath, near Tespur, on the Brahmaputra, and both Kachāri and Jaintia countries came under Ahom rule. The Jaintia people, girding under the Ahom yoke, rose two years later, and at first had some successes against the small Ahom forces left in the hills, until the garrison at Demera, in the upper Kopili valley, managing to co-operate with the troops left to hold Jaintiapur, the Ahoms overcame all resistance and finally ended the campaign in a drastic manner with a great massacre at, and the destruction of the city of Jaintiapur. A little later Rudra Sing released his two royal captives at a big durbar held at Sālāgarh, opposite to Bishnath, and allowed them to return to their own States, which, however, remained feudatory to the Ahoms. Exhausted by this last war, the Kachāris enjoyed a period of peace for nearly a hundred years, until, in 1803, the great Moamaria rebellion in upper Assam having started against Ahom rule, the Kachāris were induced to side with the rebels, hoping thus to regain their old independence. A desultory war dragged on for two years, until the Kachāris were severely beaten in a pitched battle at Doboka, on the Jamūna river, and retired to Maibong and Cachar till 1817, when irruptions of the Manipuris under their Raja Manjit practically placed the following year the whole of Cachar and its hill district under Manipuri domination. But only for a short time, for these in their turn were in 1819–20 ousted by the Burmese, who, conquering the State of Manipur, soon had Cachar in their hands, which they held till their aggressions generally at Rangoon, as well as in Assam, caused the English to declare war upon them, and their ejection from Assam speedily followed. The first visit to Khāspur, in Cachar, of any Englishman at all events any one of note, is that recorded in 1763 by Mr. Verelst from Bengal, who later became Governor-General; while the first recorded hostility between the British and the people of this locality, namely the vicinity of Cachar, was that which took place between a detachment of the Honourable East India Company's troops from Dacca and the Jaintia Raja's forces at a place twenty-one miles north-north-east of Sylhet. The Kachāris, as a nation, have now dwindled into the agricultural communities dwelling in Cachar and scattered about upper Assam; while Maibong and the North Cachar hills, so long their home and capital, have relapsed into ruins and jungle, except in the lower reaches of the Jetinga valley, which are now covered with flourishing tea gardens.

The legendary history of Kāmarupa, as Assam was called by the ancients, perpetuated in the name Kāmrup a district on the north bank of the Brahmaputra, would show the Hindu Khettri conquerors having dominated it and having in their turn given way to the Pal dynasty, and we are brought to the first authentic information to hand of this country by the Chinese traveller, Huien Tsiang, in 603 A.D. This has been touched on before, so we begin the history of the great Kocch tribe at the rise of one Shankaldip, a Kocch chief, as we have the statements of a Hindu historian and the poet Firdusi, which give a better semblance of facts than do the legendary ideas of Bisoo, whom local tradition asserts to be the founder of this dynasty. Shankaldip rose to power in the middle of the fifth century, and when Huien Tsiang visited Assam the kingdom of Kāmarupa apparently extended from the Karatoya river, near Julpigori, as far as Sadiya along the north bank of the Brahmaputra, where, it seems, the Kocch people lived amicably with the Chutiyas, who even then may have been deteriorating from having been once a powerful community. Bryan Hodgson, in his work on the Kocch and Bodo people, states that these were the most numerous and powerful aborigines in north and north-western Bengal, and the only ones who, after the Aryan ascendancy had been established, were able to retain political power or possession in the plains. A translation of the Yogini Tantra shows these people to be spoken of as Mleccha or aborigines. One Hajo, he states, founded the great Kocch kingdom in the latter part of the fifteenth century, and his successors reigned for almost 200 years. Hajo, having no sons, married his daughter to a Mecch (Bodo) chief, thus uniting the aborigines and forming the Kocch dynasty, which was eventually able to withstand invasion by the Moslems, Bhootanese, and the Ahoms ; the latter holding sway then in upper Assam, while the Kocch held lower and middle Assam. Later Kocch rulers, however, cast off the Bodo alliance and began to look with greater favour on the creeds and customs of the Aryans than on their older religion of nature, namely, the worship of stars and terrene elements. They eventually took to Hinduism, calling their country Behar, and declaring themselves to be Rājbansis. This change only affected the higher and wealthier grades of society, the masses, strange to say, mostly adopting Mahomedanism. What may have been the condition of the Kocch in the palmy days of Hinduism cannot now be ascertained, but it is certain that after the Moslem had succeeded the Hindu suzerainty, this people became so important that a Mahomedan historian, Abdul Fazul, could allude to Bengal as being " bounded on the north by the Kocch kingdom," which, he adds, " includes Kāmarupa." In 1773 this Kocch Raj was absorbed by the Great Company. Bryan Hodgson says, in speaking of their character, that they display no military or adventurous genius, but are better suited to the homely, tranquil affairs of agriculture. It is chiefly from old Moghul records of bygone invasions that any knowledge is arrived at of the Kocch people, plus lists of names of kings recorded on copper plates up to the beginning of the thirteenth century; and the earliest of these invasions was that of Mahmoud Bakhtiyar, who, desiring to conquer Thibet and deeming an easier route there to lie through the Bhootan hills, led an army in 1198 through the western end of Kāmarupa unopposed. When he had penetrated into the hills some sixteen marches, difficulties of supplies set in; he met the Thibetans in force, was beaten back, and had to conduct a disastrous retreat with the Kocch people now in arms harassing his flanks and cutting off supplies. Mahmoud eventually, with a small following, reached Dinajpore, the rest of his army having perished. In 1253 Gyasuddin, a Moghul governor of Bengal, is said to have entered and traversed Kāmarupa almost to Sadiya, but was eventually beaten back and had to retreat to Gaur. Twenty-five years later a Moghul noble, Tugril Khan, entered the Kocch country, but was almost immediately killed in battle, and his force dispersed; while in 1337, another Moghul invasion took place in the reign of Mahomed Shah Tughlak, which did not advance far into the country before it too suffered a series of defeats, and was almost entirely annihilated. The Moghul historian Ferishta's account of this invasion of China which, passing through Cooch Behar, attempted the passage of the Bhootan hills, runs as follows: "Having heard of the great wealth of China, Mahomed Tughlak conceived the idea of subduing that empire; but in order to accomplish his design it was necessary to first conquer the country of Hemachal (Nepal) and Thibet lying between the borders of China and India. Accordingly in 1337 he ordered a force of 100,000 men to subdue this mountain region under his sister's son, Khoosroo Mulk, and to establish garrisons as far as the border of China. When this was effected he proposed to advance in person with his whole army to invade that empire. Nobles and state councillors in vain assured him that the troops of India never yet could, and never would, advance a step within the limits of China, and that the whole scheme was visionary. The king insisted on making the experiment, and the army was put in motion. Having entered the mountains, small forts were built on the road to secure communications, and proceeding in this manner the troops reached the

Chinese border, where a numerous army appeared to oppose them. The numbers of the Indians were at this time greatly diminished, and being much inferior to the enemy they were struck with dismay, which was only increased when they realised their distance from home, the rugged nature of the country they had passed, the approach of the rainy season, and the scarcity of provisions which was now badly felt. With these feelings they commenced their retreat to the foot of the range of hills, where the mountaineers, rushing down upon them, plundered their baggage, and the Chinese army also followed them closely. In this distressing situation the Indian troops remained seven days, suffering greatly from famine. At length the rain began to fall in torrents and the cavalry were up to the bellies of their horses in water. The rains obliged the Chinese to move their camp to a greater distance, and gave Khoosroo Mulk some hopes of effecting his retreat ; but he found the low country completely inundated, and the mountains covered with impervious woods. The misfortunes of the army seemed to be at a crisis ; no passage remained to them for retreat but that by which they had entered the hills, and which was now occupied by the mountaineers. So that in the short space of fifteen days the Indian army fell a prey to famine, and became the victims of the king's ambition. Scarcely a man returned to relate the particulars excepting some of those left behind in the garrisons below, and the few of those troops who evaded the enemy did not escape the more fatal vengeance of the king, who ordered them to be put to death on their return to Delhi." Mahomed later sent another army to avenge the loss of the first ;

but its officers on arrival at the Kocch confines flatly refused to cross the border into a " land of witchcraft and magic." This all goes to prove that the Kocch people were a powerful nation and well versed in the arts of war of those times ; but beyond these bare military records of the Moghuls we can get at no detailed information of these people till the reign of Nar Narain, who flourished from 1515 on. This king, who reigned fifty years, an exceptionally long time for an Asiatic ruler, built what is now Cooch Behar in substitution for the old city of Kamātāpur, which had been destroyed by the later Moghul invasions ; and in 1546 began the long series of wars against the rising power of the Ahoms in the extreme east of upper Assam. Minor struggles had occurred between the two peoples from 1332, but with Ahom power now established, matters took a far more serious turn. With the aid of his famous general, Silarai, the Ahoms were worsted on the Dikrai river and at Koliabar (in Nowgong district) ; and the following year Silarai captured Narainpur on the north bank of the Brahmaputra, and Nar Narain completed the great raised roadway of 350 miles, called the Kamali Alli, connecting this town, where a fort was being built, with Cooch Behar, many parts of which are still in existence and use. Major Hannay is of opinion, however, that a road had existed ages before Nar Narain's reign, which connected the old cities east of Sadiya with the more flourishing western districts of upper Assam, and by which pilgrims were able to visit the sacred shrines of " Tāmasāri Mai " and " Bora Bhoori " near Sadiya. In 1562 Nar Narain again attacked the Ahoms with such success that he captured their capital

Garhgaon, in the neighbourhood of the present Sibsagor, and retired to his own province with an immense amount of loot. Six years later the western part of the Kocch kingdom was invaded by the Moghuls under Suleiman Kararāni, and Nar Narain's forces sustained several crushing defeats. Gauhati, then a large, flourishing city on both banks of the Brahma-

"Umanand" or Peacock Island opposite Gauhati.

putra, was taken and looted, while a notorious Brahmin renegade, one of Suleiman's suite, namely Kala Pahar, was allowed to work his iconoclastic tendencies on the ancient Kāmakhya and other famous temples, which he more or less demolished. Some years later these were rebuilt by Nar Narain. In 1578 this king, deeming it well to be on good terms with the Moghul power, sent an embassy with presents as far as Agra, where it was well received by the

Emperor Akhbar. Nar Narain's reign saw the rise of a new form of Hindu religion preached by a reformer, Sankar Deb, whose tenets were based on a purified Vishnuism, which it was hoped might supplant the Tantric form of Hinduism, for ages the prevailing religion among the Kocch people. The subject of religion will be dealt with later. In the next reign, which brings us up to the end of the sixteenth century, we see the Kocch dominions comprise the country from the Karatoya to the Sankosh rivers and the districts now known as Kāmrup and Mangaldai on the north bank, together with Goalpāra and Mymensing on the south bank of the Brahmaputra; and that their ruler must have been powerful is shown in the "Akhbarnamah" of that time, when King Lakshmi Narain declares himself to be a vassal of the Moghul Emperor, and wherein it is stated the Kocch king's forces numbered 40,000 horse, 200,000 foot soldiers, 700 elephants, and 1,000 ships. In the legends connecting one Bisoo as the originator of the Kocch kings it is said that he, at the height of his prosperity, caused a census to be taken and found that he had over 5,000,000 men fit to bear arms. This, though, of course, unreliable, together with the authentic information of the "Akhbarnamah," gives a good idea of the populous state of this country—only a part of Assam; more especially when one compares it with the census of 1901, which showed that the entire population of the Assam valley was only a little over two and a half millions. In 1612, as the result of a quarrel between the Kocch king and the Nawab of Dacca, the latter crossed the Karatoya with a force of 6,000 horse, 11,000 foot, and a fleet of 500 ships on the

Brahmaputra filled with soldiers, and laid siege to Dhubri, which would seem to have been an important and well-defended place in those days, for it held out against this force for a month. Shortly after this, the Kocch king dying, opposition in his country ceased, and the Mahomedans annexed in the name of the emperor Jehangir the country up to the Bār Naddi, which flows through the present Mangaldai district, with the exception of the country between the Karatoya and Sankōsh rivers, to which the Kocch kings were now restricted, until by the middle of the eighteenth century this too had come under Mahomedan rule. It eventually passed into British possession in 1765 on Bengal falling into English hands, and the present small State of Cooch Behar represents all that is left of the once powerful Kocch kingdom.

CHAPTER III

We now come to the last of the three great powers in upper Assam, who being a more or less literate people, have given us through their well connected historical records, or " buranjis " written in the Pali character, the clearest knowledge of doings in that country, whether touching on the Kocches, Kachāris or Moghuls, during their 600 years of power. As mentioned before, the Ahoms, whose " h " softened to " s," has given us the name " Assam," were non-Buddhist Shans, by religion pagans and demon worshippers, who, trekking west from their own country, of which Mogoung, in upper Burma, was the capital, in the early part of the thirteenth century reached the eastern extremity of the Brahmaputra valley and formed settlements in the Nāmrup locality on the Dihing river. Their immediate neighbours were then the Chutiya tribe, who ruled the country east of the Subansiri river, and the Moran tribe, between the Dikkoo and Dihing rivers. With the latter they soon came into conflict, and by 1236 the Ahoms had established themselves at and around Abhaypur, while twenty years later saw them in occupation of the country near Charaideo, which they made their capital ; and which, in spite of its removal later on to

Garhgaon, for several hundred years was a place of importance and sanctity to the Ahom kings, many of whom were buried there, while the heads of conquered chiefs and notables were invariably interred on Charaideo hill. A similar custom obtained amongst the Manipuris and the Tangkul Nagas who both, up to modern times, buried their enemies' heads in special localities. By the end of the thirteenth century they had been much strengthened by a fresh

THE DIBONG WHERE IT LEAVES THE HILLS.

trek of emigrants from across the Patkoi range and had come into conflict with the Kachāri people, whose north-eastern border was the Dikkoo river. Fifty years later saw the commencement of the long continued series of struggles between the Ahoms and Kocches. In 1380 they crushed the Chutiya power across the Brahmaputra, and a few years later changed the capital from Charaideo to Charguja, near the Dihing river, which brought about hostilities with the Tipam tribe, whose lands they now occupied. The first

Ahom record of Mahomedan efforts in the direction of upper Assam is in 1401, which shows how far west the Ahoms were then dwelling, when the Moghul forces, coming up by river, reached Koliabar nearly opposite Tezpur, where they met the Ahom forces, and being defeated there on land and water, were pursued to far below Goalpāra. The end of this century saw the defeat of the Kachāris on the Dikkoo at Dampuk, and the early part of the sixteenth century the subjugation of the Chutiya tribe and the annexation of their country, after severe fighting near Sadiya and at Kaitāra hill, said to be in the vicinity of the mouth of the Dibong river. By now the Ahoms had consolidated their power in what is now Lakhimpur on the north, and as far west as Golaghat on the south bank of the Brahmaputra. In 1526 the Ahoms drove back the Kachāris who objected to the building of the strong fort at Marangi (Moriani ?) almost on their borderland, and ascending the Dhansiri river they fought two successful engagements at Bardua and Maiham (unidentified) when the Kachāris gave in. The following year saw the Ahoms defeating another Mahomedan invasion near Duimunisila, where a fort was built and garrisoned. In this fight is the first record of weapons other than what were then generally used, namely, bows and arrows, spears, axes, etc., when forty Moghul cannon were captured. Five years later found the Ahoms not only successfully beating the Kachāris in the Dhansiri valley and dictating terms at their capital of Dimāpur, but also repelling another Moghul invasion below Koliabar, which led to their placing a large garrison as low down as Singiri, a little north of Gauhati on the north bank and close to the Kocch border. This period appears to have been one of little peace and rest for the Ahoms who next year, 1532, had again to withstand an invasion by Turbak Khan, a Moghul noble, who with a large fleet sailed up the Brahmaputra to Singiri, where he defeated the Ahom army which retired to Sālāgarh on the south bank. Turbak again successfully attacked Sālāgarh and moved further east; when luck turning, favoured his enemy. The Ahom king sending large reinforcements by land and river was at last successful; and in a heavy battle again at Duimunisila Turbak's forces were defeated, he himself killed, and his head, as was customary, sent for burial on Charaideo hill. The beaten and disorganised forces were pursued by the victorious Ahoms through Kocch territory to the Karatoya river. At the Duimunisila fight the recorded Mahomedan losses were over 2,500 men, twenty-two ships, and many big guns; so that with the losses in the pursuit the Moghul casualty list must have been a long one; while the booty that fell to the pursuers is stated to have been twenty-eight elephants, a great number of guns and matchlocks, with a quantity of gold and silver ornaments and utensils. It is now that we find the Ahoms taking to fire-arms and utilising the numbers captured from the Moghuls in preference to bows and spears. It is supposed that they were taught their use and the rough manufacture of powder by their Mahomedan prisoners, and certainly by the time of Mir Jumla's famous invasion of a century later, or about 1662, they were proficient in the art of forging iron for cannon, of making excellent powder, and of intelligently using the same; which is vouched for by the old time French traveller, Tavernier. It is in 1536 that the Ahom "buranjis" first mention trouble with any of the wild hill tribes

A Trans Dikkoo Naga in War Paint and one from Tabhlung.

who inhabit the mountains which hem in upper Assam, and we now find the Khāmjang, Nāmsang, and Tabhlung Nagas raiding into the plains and standing up to the trained Ahoms in fights, in one of which the two latter tribes not only inflicted severe loss but captured several guns before they finally submitted. This argues a higher form of bravery and fighting to what we are accustomed to find in these wild tribes, and also that their village communities must have been far more powerful than those of the present day; for these three tribes are well known, the head villages of Nāmsang and Tabhlung lying only a few miles east and south of our present military police outpost of Tamlu in the Naga hills, where the Dikkoo river makes its exit from the mountains. A year later the Ahoms are found defeating the Kachāris in the Doyang and Dhansiri valleys, and sacking their ancient capital of Dimāpur. The destruction of this and their heavy losses took all heart out of the Kachāri people, who, as we have seen before, evacuated the Dhansiri valley and formed a new capital at Maibong in what is now called the North Cachar hills. For what reason the Ahoms never occupied this part of Kachāri territory is not known, but as it was quite depopulated by war it soon relapsed into a jungle too heavy perhaps for the conquerors to cope with; and so it developed into the dense Nambhor forest, gradually covering and blotting out all evidences of Kachāri towns, roads, etc., which had been their pride and home for hundreds of years. This reign, namely that of Sūkmūngnūng lasting forty-two years, was long and eventful. It was notable for successful military operations which ended in the subjugation of the Chutiyas and Kachāris, while three Moghul invasions were repulsed. The social condition of the people was also considerably attended to, and artisans from Bengal imported to teach arts and crafts, while firearms were also introduced. This latter fact is all the more remarkable and interesting seeing that, 120 years before, artillery and hand guns had not emerged from their very elementary condition in Europe, and indeed were only beginning to be generally used in war about the middle of the fifteenth century. The official capital was in this reign moved to Garhgaon not far from Sibsagor, and about 1552 the big tank there was excavated by the Ahom king, Sukhlemning, who also was the first to strike coins, and who also built the raised roadway called the Naga Alli, running from the Baralli to the Naga hills. The year 1546, as we have seen before, found the Ahoms at war with Nar Narain, the most powerful monarch in this part of India, and the Kocch arms at first very successful; but later, the Ahoms getting the upper hand, the war subsided owing to the exhaustion of both forces. Before the sixteenth century was out the Ahoms had to deal with an invasion by the Kocch king, Nar Narain, who successfully captured the strong Ahom positions at Boka, Sālāgarh, and Handia, chiefly by means of a strong fleet on the river. The occupation of their capital Garhgaon by Nar Narain, caused the Ahoms to cede Narainpur on the north bank to the Kocches, who closed the war and hurried back to repel a Moghul invasion in which, being unsuccessful, Nar Narain released all the Ahom hostages, hoping thereby to gain their friendship and alliance. This, however, did not come off, as the Ahoms were too busy in dealing not only with the Chutiya people, who were once more in revolt, but also with the Nārā Raja of Mayankwan, beyond the Patkoi range. The seventeenth century opened for this nation in further trouble with the Kachāris, and severe actions took place at Dharmtika and Rạhā, involving heavy losses on both sides; at the latter place the Ahoms being severely beaten. A few years later, namely in 1615, the Moghul governor of Bengal despatched Aba Bakr with a force of 10,000 troops and 400 ships against the Ahom king. These arrived in due time at Hajo, a few miles from the river on its north bank and opposite Gauhati without opposition; and making Hajo their base they advanced to meet their enemies on the Bharali river. After a stiff encounter Aba Bakr was victorious; but failing to reap the full advantage of his success by pursuing vigorously, the Ahom king was able to send up large reinforcements. The battle was renewed, Aba Bakr killed, and his force driven back on Hajo. Here the Ahoms were joined by various petty Rajas and their following, all anxious to be rid of the Mahomedan invaders. These managed to capture the Moghul position at Pandoo, near Gauhati, while the main Ahom army was hemming in the Moghuls at Hajo. After six weeks a battle was brought on by the Ahoms, ending in the complete discomfiture of the invaders and their dispersal with heavy loss; the latter including many horses, cannon, and cattle, which fell into the victors hands. Twenty years later the Mahomedans were again at Hajo with the friendly connivance of the Kocches, and as their presence caused continual friction in this part of the country, the Ahom king, Pratap Sing, was induced to declare war on them; when, after defeating them at Niubihan he invested Hajo. In other parts of the district, namely, at Pandoo and Srighat, Ahom troops were not so successful; but more men and ships arriving, the Moghuls were driven from Pandoo and almost annihilated at Sualkuchi, on the north bank, a little below Pandoo, 300 ships and many cannon and matchlocks being captured. Curiously enough, the Ahom records of this fight make the first mention of any European being in Assam, when amongst their prisoners they found a Feringhi, but of what nationality is not known. Ralph Fitche, a merchant in Queen Elizabeth's time, had visited Kamātāpur, the Kocch capital, but no European had gone further east. Having cleared the Moghuls off the river, the Ahoms concentrated for the assault of Hajo, which fell after a desperate defence, when an immense amount of loot, munitions of war, etc., were secured. Pratap Sing, pursuing his advantage, continued his advance down river, seizing all Mahomedan posts as far as Goalpāra. This continuance of success for the Ahoms was not of long duration, for almost immediately the Nawab of Dacca despatched a force of 12,000 men to recover the territory thus lost to Bengal, and it was not long before he captured a strong fort at Jogighopa, near the mouth of the Manās river, from which he secured the submission of the Goalpāra country opposite. The Ahoms, beaten at Jogighopa, drew off to the foot of the Bhootan hills and awaited reinforcements. These arrived duly, and with 40,000 men they attacked the Moghuls in their camp at Bishenpur. In the heavy battle that ensued Pratap Sing's troops were beaten with the loss of over 4,000 men and several generals. A later defeat in a naval action on the Brahmaputra at Srighat, followed by the capture of Pandoo and Gauhati, placed the whole of Kāmārupa for the time being at the Moghul disposal, whose commander made his headquarters at Gauhati and began to consolidate his rule. The Kocches having joined the Moghuls in this war, it was not long before the Ahoms retaliated by attacking their troops on the Bharāli river, whom they pursued almost to Gauhati. Here, as the resources of both belligerents were almost down to nil after a war extending to almost three years, peace was made; and the Bar Naddi, running into the Brahmaputra opposite Gauhati, became the eastern boundary of Mahomedan possessions. This brings one to the end of King Pratap Sing's reign, as he died in 1641, after thirty-eight eventful years, during which two great wars had been conducted against the Kachāris and the Moghuls, although not always with uniform success to the Ahoms. Great attention had been paid to internal organisation, markets were established and trade fostered. Buildings of masonry and of a permanent nature were erected, notably at Abhaypur, Mathurapur, and Garhgaon, the latter being fortified and having a palace built in its centre, the ruins of which are still visible. The Ahom capital Garhgaon is described in the "buranjis" of that time as being "of great size with the palace in the centre, the city was surrounded by a well-raised solid embankment serving instead of customary fortifications, and on the top of which ran a roadway. In this embankment were four masonry gates each three kōs (a kōs is one and a quarter miles) from the palace, which again was defended by a deep ditch and stockade work of great strength. The palace was of masonry, and the audience hall therein is said to be 120 cubits by 36 cubits." Of the state of the country in this part of

Assam at this period it is described as being "on the north bank (*i.e.*, what is now north Lakhimpur) more under cultivation than about Garhgaon, but generally on the south bank as far down as Koliabar were extensive fields and fine rice crops." Wild elephants are said to have been exceedingly numerous, 160 being caught in one drive in 1654. King Pratap Sing also constructed many roads and tanks, threw up the great Dopgarh embankment as a protection against Naga inroads, and developed backward tracts. He built the forts at Samdhāra, Safrai, and Sila, while several stone bridges are believed to date from his reign. This king, having been the first to be converted to Hinduism, which occurred about 1613, later many nobles following his example, Brahmin influence soon became powerful and many Hindus from India were given high official posts. The Ahom language was, however, still predominant. Although no longer the official capital, Charaideo maintained its sacred interest. Ahom kings worshipped, buried the heads of the eminent persons killed in battle on the hill overlooking Charaideo, and were mostly buried there themselves. These tombs were covered with large mounds, and the royal funeral customs prescribed that the queen, certain guards, slaves, and an elephant or a horse, should be buried with deceased royalty. Some of these mounds have been opened and from the spaces inside, bones and ornaments found, it is conjectured the above customs were really observed. The next fifteen years saw the Ahoms worried by incursions of the Daphlas and Mirris on the north bank of the Brahmaputra, which were put down drastically and many of the villages burnt; while on the south bank the Lakma Nagas in the hills south-east of Sibsagor, between the Dilli and Dikkoo rivers, appeared to have been sufficiently strong to carry on a series of raids into the plains and to seriously harass the Ahom troops sent into the hills against them.

These particular Nagas were visited in February, 1900, by the Deputy Commissioner with a punitive party, and were found to be anything but a war-like people. In 1658, owing to confusion arising in Bengal consequent on the Emperor Shah Jehan's illness, the Kocch people rose and made a supreme effort to throw off the Moghul yoke under which for years they had lain. The Ahoms were induced to join in this, and while the Kocches overpowered the Moghuls in Goalpāra and southern Kāmarupa, their allies proceeded against and captured Hajo and Gauhati. Dissensions, however, arising between the two allies, the Ahoms attacked and drove the Kocches across the Sankosh river, which joins the Brahmaputra at Dubhri, after which they became masters of entire Assam. A mastery which they only enjoyed four years, for 1662 saw the Moghul armies again in motion under Mir Jumla, then Governor of Bengal, to recover the lost territory. As this is the most famous of all Moghul invasions it is deserving of more attention and in greater detail.

CHAPTER IV

MIR JUMLA, who was Moghul Governor of Bengal, moved to Dacca where, with the Nawab, he organised a force of 12,000 horse, 30,000 foot, and a large fleet of boats ; and proceeding early in 1662 along the north bank of the river, arrived at Dhubri, which the Ahom troops vacated in favour of the strong fort of Jogighopa at the mouth of the Manās river. The Moghul strength was too much for the Ahom garrison of 12,000, who, after a short siege, cut their way out and retired on Srighat and Pandoo on either side of the Brahmaputra close to Gauhati, which were fortified.

On this Mir Jumla divided his army, sending one wing over to the south bank while he with the other proceeded along the north bank. His fleet of three hundred boats, many of which were very large, styled "Gharabs," so called from their swiftness, sombre appearance of sail and hull, and from the Arabic word "ghorab," a raven, and mounting fourteen cannon and sixty to seventy soldiers, which records state to have been in charge of European officers, presumably Portuguese, proceeded up river between the two wings, the whole presenting the most formidable array of force that had yet entered Assam. On nearing the defile of the Brahmaputra below Gauhati

Mir Jumla manœuvred the Ahoms out of Pandoo and Srighat and occupied Gauhati after the storming of one small fort at Beltola. As the Ahoms had now retired to Samdhāra above Tezpur at the mouth of the Bharāli river, and to Simlagarh almost opposite on the south bank, the Moghuls rested awhile at Gauhati and reconnoitred. This resulted in Mir Jumla bringing over the northern wing to the south bank, the crossing being effected at Tezpur; and with his whole army and fleet moved against Simlagarh, a large earthwork fort mounting many cannon. The strength of the place precluded the possibility of a direct assault, so it was regularly besieged. But after a short siege Mir Jumla's patience gave out on finding his cannon produced no effect on the thick earth walls —an experience which had its counterpart in Lord Lake's and Lord Combermere's famous sieges of Bhurtpore,—and he ordered the place to be stormed. Had the Ahom troops been well led the Moghuls could have been easily repulsed; as it was the assault, involving considerable losses, succeeded. The discomfited Ahoms vacated Samdhāra, not without, however, putting up a good fight at Koliabar on land and river, where, losing nearly 200 ships and many men and guns, a general retirement on Garhgaon the capital, took place, pursued by the Moghul horse. As it seemed to the Ahom king impossible to stop the victorious advance of Mir Jumla, he vacated the capital and retired first to Charaideo and thence to Nāmrup on the Dilli river, the most easterly point of the Ahom dominions. On the 17th of March, 1662, Mir Jumla's army occupied Garhgaon, securing, owing to the hasty retreat of the Ahoms, considerable booty, namely, three lakhs of rupees in gold and silver, 170 storehouses full of rice, and eighty-two elephants. Here the army rested and again reconnoitred; but the rains setting in early brought the commencement of trouble to the invaders. Garhgaon proving unhealthy, Mir Jumla moved his army to Mathurapur, near Charaideo, which stood on slightly higher land, and there, after establishing certain posts to overawe the surrounding country, the invaders awaited the return of seasonable weather. But not in peace; for the Ahom king, realising the discomfort and straits of his enemy, rallied his forces and directed attacks against the Moghul posts with success; for these one after another were overwhelmed, obliging Mir Jumla to concentrate all his force in and around Mathurapur, where dysentery and fever soon began to thin his ranks. Several Ahom attacks were with great difficulty repulsed; and news now reached Mir Jumla to the effect that the Kocch people, hearing of his trouble, had seized the opportunity of rising *en masse* behind him and had overthrown all Moghul garrisons which had been stationed on the north bank in Kāmarupa. After the rains had cleared off, certain Moghul reinforcements managed to reach him by river with the serious news of a famine in Bengal, and that after this no further supplies of any sort were possible from that country. Mir Jumla was now ailing with fever, and seeing any further stay in the country or successful hostilities against the Ahoms to be impossible, he concluded peace and began a retreat, which as it went on was conducted in the greatest misery. It had been Mir Jumla's intention to deal with the rebellious Kocches on his way back, but his own serious illness and discontent among his troops rendered any attempts of this sort out of the question; and the shattered Moghul forces which had opened the invasion so brilliantly reached the confines of Bengal in March, 1663, Mir Jumla dying just before Dacca was reached. The Indian campaigns in those far off days seem always to have been conducted on stupendous lines; and the present day mind can scarcely conjure up the spectacle of these great battles in the neighbourhood of Gauhati and Tezpur, with many thousands engaged and the river covered with several hundreds of warships as well joining in! How Mir Jumla marched and manœuvred his forty odd thousand troops by land is not stated, but considering there must have been thousands of camp followers as well, the whole operations are indeed wonderful, particularly so when compared with the great difficulties we have always experienced in moving a few hundred troops about Assam in all the little border operations that have occurred since we came on the scene there. Moghul writers at that time speak of the river traffic and commerce on the Brahmaputra as being very heavy, while the Ahom war boats were numerous and all mounted cannon; which shows the condition of prosperity and strength to which that nation had attained in the middle of the seventeenth century. It would appear, however, that according to Mir Jumla's treaty of peace, Moghul garrisons were left in Gauhati until the payment of the war indemnity had been settled in full by the Ahoms, whose new king refused the demands made by Firoz Khan to settle up completely. This refusal started the war again in 1667, and an Ahom army marched down both banks of the Brahmaputra on Gauhati where, after one reverse on the Bar Naddi, they succeeded in besieging both the Gauhati and Pandoo garrisons, which gave in after a two months' siege and much fighting. Many cannon fell into Ahom hands. The remaining Moghul troops, retiring on the Manās river, they were eventually surrounded and cut up entirely, Firoz Khan being captured with most of his officers. At Silghat and Dikom, near Dibrugarh, are still to be seen two old Moghul cannon taken in this campaign, with dates and inscriptions on them. Aurangzeb, then emperor at Delhi, naturally did not allow these successes of the Ahom king, Chakradhoj, to pass unnoticed; for the year following he ordered one of his generals, Raja Ram Singh, to fit out a force of 18,000 horse and 30,000 foot to punish the Ahoms for the defeat of his last army. These advanced from Bengal in the open season of 1668, and *en route* were joined by 15,000 Kocch allies. Much fighting occurred in the vicinity of Tezpur where at first the Ahoms were beaten, but rallying a little got the upper hand and forced the Moghul troops back on Hajo. In this neighbourhood as well as on the Sessa river, success varied between each side, until at the end of the year both armies, wearied with their efforts, began to negociate, and hostilities being suspended, Ram Singh vacated Assam, having generally had the worst of it. The year 1673 saw the Daphla tribes in revolt, which was put down with some difficulty, and not before one force of Ahoms was surrounded and destroyed.

Chakradhoj's reign, which ended late in 1673, was

chiefly remarkable for the eviction of all Moghuls from Kāmarupa (or Central Assam), and the strong fortifications erected by him at Gauhati on both sides of the Brahmaputra. He also established several foundries capable of turning out numbers of cannon for his force. The next ten years were not those of progress for the Ahoms, for the nation was distracted by many internecine wars between members of the nobility which impoverished the country. Seven kings in this short period were set up and either died or were murdered, and all was chaos until at last a strong ruler, Gadardhar Sing, arose, who, however, only reigned nine years, in which time he was successful in ridding his kingdom entirely of the Moghuls and stipulating in the final treaty that the Manās river should become the boundary between the two countries. This left the Kocch country entirely under Moghul suzerainty. He also put down with drastic severity a number of Naga and Mirri raids, built the picturesque temple on Peacock Island opposite Gauhati, and made the two highways, the Dhodar and Aka Allis, the former of which is still in use between Jorhat and Charaideo, and still further here and there. Religion in his reign did not make for peace, for the Vishnubite sect were getting too much power into their hands, which he found necessary to reduce by continuous persecution. The system of land measurements as used by the Moghuls was also introduced by him. Rudra Sing, who succeeded Gadardhar and reigned eighteen years, is generally regarded as the greatest of all the Ahom kings, and rightly so, when we consider what he accomplished; namely, improvements in communications through his country and the construction of numerous masonry bridges, the erection of brick buildings at Rangpur and Charaideo with the aid of Kocch artisans, the conquering of the Kachāris and Jaintias for good and all, the reception of the submission of all hill tribes, the establishment of extensive trade with Thibet, the importation of artificers from Bengal, and the establishment of intercourse with other nations to whom envoys were sent. He also started the system of schools for Brahmins, as in later life he became an orthodox Hindu.

His trouble with the Kachāris began early in 1696, and at the close of that year he equipped two armies to settle the dispute. The strongest of 37,000 men was sent against the Kachāri capital, Maibong (in the now North Cachar hills) viâ the Dhansiri valley, to Mohun Dijoa; the other army of 34,000 moved viâ Rāhā in the Nowgong district up the Kopili valley. The first force, after an action at Dijoa, reached Maibong, and, defeating the Kachāris outside, captured the town and destroyed its walls and defences. The second force, arriving late owing to great difficulties in cutting its way through the dense forest on the upper Kopili, was ordered to press on through the hills to seize Khāspur, the next city of importance to the Kachāris and which after this became the capital, in the plains of Silchar. But shortage of food and sickness breaking out in the army, obliged Rudra Sing to content himself with what he had so far achieved, and the Ahoms retired. Nine years later the Kachāris got into difficulties with their neighbours, the Jaintias, who occupy all the hill country in the centre of which lies the present station of Shillong; and after several small engagements the Jaintia Raja succeeded, through treachery, in capturing Tamradhoj the Kachāri king, whose ministers appealed to Rudra Sing for assistance against their enemies. The Ahom king, responding, sent two forces against the Jaintias, one of which, passing through the hills, occupied the capital, Jaintiapur; the other column, having more opposition to overcome, did not get as far. Tamradhoj was released, the Jaintia Raja taken prisoner, and Rudra Sing now formally annexed the Jaintia and Kachāri countries to his own, leaving garrisons behind to enforce his rule. As Tamradhoj objected to this annexation he was kept a prisoner in the Ahom camp, and, with the Jaintia king, was sent back to Bishnath, a little above Tezpur. The Jaintia people, aided in a small way by the Kachāris, made supreme efforts to shake off Ahom rule during 1708, and at first with some success, until the Ahom troops, stationed at Demera in the upper Kopili valley, managed to cooperate with those holding Jaintiapur on the south side of the hills; and, with the loss of nearly 3,000 men and twelve high officials, overcame resistance; finally restoring order after a great massacre at, and the total destruction of Jaintiapur, where an immense amount of loot was taken. There are Ahom records of their losses in this war, showing the extent of their military resources, from which we find that of the killed alone, 900 came from upper Assam, over 1,000 from Gauhati, and several hundreds from Sonapur and the Dekeri country. This rebellion now crushed out, Rudra Sing withdrew to Sālāgarh on the Brahmaputra opposite Bishnath, and while here held a grand Durbar, to which Tamradhoj was first called. He was conducted across the river in the royal barge, and on landing mounted an elephant with gold trappings. Rudra Sing, surrounded by his nobles and generals, received him in a magnificent " shamiana " supported by gold and silver poles, whilst masses of troops stationed around must have given an added note of power to that of the magnificence of the actual Durbar. Tamradhoj, dismounting, proceeded to the royal presence on foot where, introduced by one of the chief nobles who recited the circumstances leading up to this occasion, the captured king prostrated himself, and was immediately offered a seat by Rudra Sing, who then received his complete submission ; and shortly afterwards escorted by Ahom troops as far as Demera where the escort was changed for one from his own people, he reached Khāspur.

Rudra Sing then received Ram Sing, the Jaintia king, in somewhat similar style, but, as his nobles hesitated as to complete submission the proceedings were not marked by the friendliness shown at the first Durbar ; and before the nobles could be brought to reason Ram Sing died of dysentery. Rudra Sing dying in August, 1714, he was succeeded by his son Sib Sing, whose reign, though long (some thirty years), was uneventful, being disturbed only once by the Daphlas. Under this king Hinduism became the religion of the country ; but his queen, Phuleswari, being under the strong influence of the Sakta Hindu sect, she set her face against the Vishnubite section (the so-called Moamaria) and ordered some of their Gosains to be smeared at a Sakta shrine with the blood of sacrificial victims. The insult was never forgotten, and led to far-reaching and disastrous results later on. From this reign, with its strong religious tendencies, is to be traced the beginning of the decay of the Ahom strength; for the Brahmins forbidding the free eating of meats and strong drinks, their physique began to deteriorate, which has gone on steadily ever since. Sib Sing is said to have completed surveys of all Ahom territory, and during his reign is a record of the first visit of three Englishmen to upper Assam, whose names are given as Godwin, Lister, and Mill. The purpose of their visit, which was in 1730, is not stated. The next period of interest, namely 1765, is the Burmese invasion of Manipur, and the call by that Raja on the Ahom king, Rajeswari Sing, for aid. This was responded to by the sending of a force to Manipur from Charaideo through the hills; but it was obliged to turn back after it had got a little way in owing to the difficulties of that part of the country. A second force had, however, been assembled at Rāhā, and this, proceeding through the Kachāri country, reached Manipur where the Raja was reinstated. Beyond these bare facts there are no records as to the route taken by the Ahoms, or of any collision between them and the Burmese. The Ahom people had by now, under several good kings, become very prosperous, and had enjoyed considerable internal order; but there were not wanting signs of approaching decay in the evaporation of old warlike instincts, while continual religious sectarian disputes almost blotted out anything like patriotic ideas.

In the next reign (Lukshmi Sing's) continuous insults heaped by certain Ahom nobles on the Moamaria Gosain, or Mahanta, caused the disaffection of that sect towards the throne to become more pronounced, while the cruel persecution of this large and powerful sect drove them finally, in 1769, to open rebellion headed by the Moamaria Gosain, whose son Bāngan collected their first formed body of fighting men, and entered the district of Nāmrup in the extreme east of Assam. Their first engagement with Lukshmi Sing's troops was not successful, but later in the year another leader, Rāgha, led an insurgent body down the north bank of the Brahmaputra and succeeded in defeating the royalist forces several times, eventually capturing the Ahom king and some of his nobles, these latter being instantly put to death.

The Moamaria Gosain now caused the son of the Moran chief, Rāmakant, to be raised to the throne; but this *régime* only lasted a short while, as the royalist nobles, making a last effort to restore the old administration, managed to capture Rāgha, and later Rāmakant, who, with their families, were put to death. Lukshmi Sing was released, reinstated, and with this success followed a most rigorous persecution of the Moamaria. The Gosain and numbers of his followers were captured; and as the Ahoms had always been notorious for their cruel and revolting forms of punishment, these people were killed with indescribable tortures, ending with impalement.

CHAPTER V

THE change of sovereign on the death of Lukshmi Sing in December, 1780, did nothing to ameliorate the situation, for Gaurinath Sing was also a bitter enemy of the sect, and two years after his accession a terrible massacre of Moamaria at Garhgaon led to another prolonged revolt; and with such success for the sect, that in 1791 Gaurinath's troops having been frequently beaten, and the Moamaria having set up one of their own on the throne at Rangpur, Gaurinath applied for assistance to the Jaintia and Kachāri Rajas, who declined help. Manipur being applied to did send a force of 500 horse and 4,000 foot across the Naga hills to Nowgong, whence they moved against Rangpur; but, being badly worsted, retired to their own country. Manipur chronicles relating this action show that many of their soldiers were severely flogged and many deported for cowardice. Kāmarupa and upper Assam were now in a most miserable plight; all these years of fighting had desolated the land for both belligerents; villages were burnt, crops destroyed, and now a famine started. At this juncture Gaurinath bethought him of the English who had held the districts of Goalpāra and Cooch Behar since 1765, when the whole of the Moghul possessions in Bengal passed into their hands. A Mr. Douglas administered Cooch Behar, and Goalpāra and Jogighopa forts were both held by the English troops, Lieutenants Crump and Lennon with a company of Sepoys each, being at the latter places, all of which were under the jurisdiction of the Commissioner of the English province of Rangpur. At Goalpāra the only civilian European was a Mr. Rausch, a Hanoverian merchant dealing

THE BARAIL RANGE, ANGAMI COUNTRY, NAGA HILLS.

in the salt trade, who knew the state of affairs, and also that in the lawless state of the country gangs of mercenaries were coming over from Bengal, taking sides with either Ahoms or Moamaria, or were acting on their own and terrorising the western end of Kāmarupa. His representations backing up Gaurinath's appeal to Mr. Lumsden, Commissioner of Rangpur, reached Lord Cornwallis, the Governor-General, who, seeing the urgency of putting a period to this state of anarchy along the English border, ordered a small force into upper Assam to restore order and to reinstate the Ahom king on his throne. To this end, in September, 1792, Captain Welsh, with Lieutenants Williams, Macgregor as Force-Adjutant, and Wood as Surveyor, with six companies of Native Infantry, namely, three of his own battalion, the 16th Native Infantry, at Barrakpore, and the others from the 19th and 24th Native Infantry at Berhampore, with a British officer to each company, were despatched by boat to Assam and reached Goalpāra early in December. A little further up the river Welsh was joined by the fugitive Ahom king with a small following, and he landed some eight miles west of Gauhati which was entered unopposed. From here a message was sent to Krishna Narain of Darrang on the north bank, whose Bengali mercenaries were the chief cause of disturbance in the west of Kāmarupa ; and as he declined to come in Welsh crossed the Brahmaputra with 280 sepoys and attacked him in his position on a fortified hill, whence he finally dislodged the large gang with a loss to him of six killed, and captured forty cannon. In this action despatches say Lieutenant Macgregor greatly distinguished himself. A few days later Lieutenant Williams, with three companies, was sent into Mangaldai, where he succeeded in completely dispersing the enemy. On Welsh's return to Gauhati, having settled that trouble, which, indeed, on leaving Calcutta, was all that had been intended for the gravity of the Moamaria rising had not then been understood, Gaurinath begged him to assist in eastern Assam where the rebellion was at its worst ; and as Welsh now received a letter from Lord Cornwallis telling him to act as seemed best until more specific instructions could be given and cordially approving his conduct of affairs, Welsh remained in Gauhati until definite information as to the Moamaria could give him a line of action to follow. His presence was also requisite to back up Gaurinath's position and authority, he being about the weakest and most craven of all Ahom monarchs. The state of affairs was duly communicated to Calcutta, which took a long time in those days, and Krishna Narnain having at last tendered his submission he took oath of allegiance and was formally installed as Raja of Darrang; and Welsh having received a reinforcement of six more companies from the 16th and 24th Native Infantry, began his move into the eastern districts in October, 1793. His progress was slow, presumably to establish friendly relations with the people and to suppress the river banditti, his proceedings receiving Lord Cornwallis's approval. It was well into February, 1794, before he neared Jorhat, which had just been surrounded by the Moamaria forces. On the 11th of February, Lieutenant Macgregor with a small detachment arrived near Jorhat and sent forward a Soubedar with twenty men to reconnoitre, he following with Lieutenant Wood and fourteen Sepoys. They found the rebels attacking Jorhat from the far side, and were moving to support the Ahom garrison, when they were suddenly attacked by 2,000 rebels. The little party remained firm in spite of the odds against them, discipline and steady firing saved the situation, and the enemy drew off, leaving eighty dead behind. Macgregor's loss was only six sepoys. Welsh now hurried up from Koliabar and had his advance guard of two companies under

Lieutenant Irvine heavily attacked twelve miles from Rangpur. Beating off his assailants, the force pushed on, but was obliged to take up a defensive position at the brick bridge over the Nāmdang river for a time. Again driving off the Moamaria, Welsh occupied the city of Rangpur after an action costing him two killed and thirty-five wounded. This instance of a small force attacking a large city some twenty miles in extent furnishes a good example of the self-confidence of and the risks willingly undertaken by the early British forces and their officers in India. It is also interesting to note that practically the last stand of the Burmese in 1825 was made at this same Nāmdang bridge near Rangpur, when Lieutenant Brooke (who became Raja of Sarawak) won the battle by his spirited charge with the irregular cavalry attached to the Rangpur Levy (later the 42nd Assam Light Infantry and now the 2nd/8th Goorkha Rifles). An immense amount of loot in cattle, grain, and treasure was secured in this city, which was sold, and the money realised given in prize money to the troops—the only action of Welsh's which was disapproved of by Lord Cornwallis, although it was done with Gaurinath's full consent.

Welsh found Rangpur city to be most extensive, upwards of twenty miles round, set in miles and miles of country showing a high state of cultivation. While here they saw a body of Manipur cavalry which had just come to Gaurinath's aid in ignorance of Welsh's successful operations. Which route they travelled by is not stated, but it shows that there was a comparatively easy one through the hills between the two countries. Gaurinath had joined the force by river on the 21st of March, and at a Durbar held by Welsh, the latter asked whether his services could now be dispensed with as the Ahom king's power had been restored and his enemies dispersed. The emphatic answer was that he could not be spared; and as the Moamaria were reported to be still in some force at Bāgmāra not far off, Welsh detailed three companies to move against them.

But a new Governor-General had recently succeeded Lord Cornwallis, namely, Sir John Shore, who at once showed himself as a "peace at any price" man by putting an end to Welsh's useful presence in Assam, and ordering a cessation of all military operations and a return to India. Orders to this effect were received as the detachment was about to start for Bāgmāra, so an opportunity for further successful action was missed.

In Welsh's report to Government in February, 1794, in which he explains the condition the country is in, what he has effected and still hopes to effect, appears a series of replies to questions by the Secretary to Government; and to one where the subject of withdrawing from the country is queried, Welsh's answer is most emphatic. He says: "If we leave the country now the contest for influence, power, and independence would revive amongst the first officers of State, dependent rajas, and chiefs of districts and towns. The same confusion, devastation, and massacre would ensue. Assam would experience a state of desolation greater in proportion to the temporary restraints which British influence has now imposed on the inhumanity of the monarch, on the ambition and resentment of the chiefs, and on the vengeance of the people. Obnoxious ministers and favourites would immediately be restored to their offices. Every individual who had been observed to cultivate British friendship would flee the country, in well grounded apprehension of destruction by the ministers or their connections. Commerce would again be suppressed by the confusion that would prevail in the country; and the monarch, whose person is too sacred for assassination, would probably be compelled to abandon his kingdom."

In another part of his letter he states: "It appears to me that the British Government should continue its mediating and controlling influence, as the only means of preserving order and tranquillity." His urgent representations and the appeal of Gaurinath for the retention of Welsh and his troops whose work he cordially appreciated, were of no avail; and an order reached Welsh to return to Bengal by the 1st of July. The Assam monarch might well appraise the work of this officer and those with him, for Welsh and his little force had succeeded admirably. By his tact, judgment, and firmness, he had brought about a restoration of order and the punishment of all marauding gangs; further, he had attained the confidence of all and had put down corrupt officials. His troops had, in fact, achieved wonders in the face of overwhelming odds and obstacles.

During the operations round Rangpur, Lieutenant Creswell, left in command at Gauhati, had been obliged to cross the Brahmaputra with two companies, the 27th and one of the 16th Native Infantry, in order to break up a large gang who were terrorising the Darrang district. A severe but successful fight ensued near Culihi, wherein our losses were heavy, namely, twenty-one killed and wounded, including Lieutenant Creswell, who succumbed next day to his wound. But this action broke up the gangs of banditti and cleared Kāmrup and Darrang of their presence. In May, 1774, Welsh and his force commenced their retirement out of the country; and at the start seized one opportunity of inflicting severe punishment on the Moamaria who threatened him in force, 4,000 strong, at the Darika river. Welsh crossed the neighbouring Dikkoo river and attacked the hostile position vigorously, dispersing them with heavy loss. On the 30th of May he reached Gauhati, where he was overwhelmed with petitions to remain and continue in his good work. His account of this old capital is interesting to those who know it in these days, when little or nothing is to be seen of its former grandeur. A little over a century ago he found it a populous and large city on both banks of the Brahmaputra with extensive commerce. A rampart ran along the river front on both banks, mounting 113 cannon, while in the centre was a sort of citadel—a large, oblong enclosure with brick walls and surrounded by wet ditches. The city entrances were through fine masonry gateways, while the fortifications of Pandoo, four miles off, guarded the river approach from the west.

One hundred years later Mr. Macdonald says, in his book on Kāmrup: "Of the former glories of Gauhati, whether under Hindoo, Ahom, or Burmese rule, the only relics which remain are the mounds and extensive lines of brick fortifications which lie scattered along the Brahmaputra. Gateways existing at the end of the eighteenth century have now entirely vanished. A large proportion of the soil in the surrounding cultivated fields is composed of brick dust, mortar, and broken pottery; while carved stones and beautifully finished slabs, the remains of once noble temples, are often found beneath the surface. The numerous large tanks attesting the command of unlimited labour possessed by ancient rulers, are now choked up with weeds and jungle." Looking down on this sea of decay is the beautiful wooded Nilachal hill, crowned with its group of famous temples, very ancient and much revered still, the home of the old Tantric form of the Hindoo religion, for centuries undisturbed and dominant throughout Assam in olden days. In fact, from the prodigious ruins of public works throughout this country and the magnificent raised roads, which we have seen were constructed in different reigns, it is probable that this remote part of India in ancient times enjoyed a superior form of government to any it has since experienced, until taken over by the English. Welsh and his force eventually reached Bengal territory on the 3rd of July, but they left behind them in the Ahom mind a realisation of what discipline and training means to troops, for Gaurinath had secured the services of two of Welsh's native officers, who, under heavy bribes, elected to serve the Ahoms. Taking the pick of all his best soldiery, Gaurinath dressed and equipped them with flint-locks; and with the aid of these two officers trained them and maintained a standing army, with which for some time he was able to hold his own against the Moamaria. But all that Welsh had prophesied to Government was soon realised on vacation of Assam by the British. The Moamaria when they once became aware of the fact that Welsh had left for good, captured Rangpur, Gaurinath fleeing to Jorhat; confusion and chaos set in, signalised by the most brutal treatment of rebels when caught, and also of those who had been befriended by Welsh. The country was devastated by war and vindictive retaliatory measures by either party, until the death, in December, 1794, of Gaurinath—the most incompetent and disreputable of all the Ahom monarchs.

He was succeeded by Kamaleshwar, whose reign of fifteen years was troubled by a rebellion in Kāmarupa fostered by the Kocch ruler, who with the Raja of Bijni moved troops into the district. With these were bands of Punjabis and Mahomedans, and every effort was made to seize this portion of the country. Kamaleshwar's more disciplined forces, however, put down the rising and expelled the invaders. Mr. Rausch (who was mentioned before) while trading on the north bank was killed by a band of these Mahomedans. As at this time the Daphlas showed signs of joining the rebellion, Ahom troops were sent into their hills, and the disaffection of this tribe was dealt with in so drastic and ruthless a manner that further trouble from them was rendered impossible. In 1799 another serious rising of the Moamaria was quickly quelled with much bloodshed, and in 1803 a short war with the Kachāri king took place, which ended in favour of the Ahoms in one battle at Doboka on the Jamūna river.

CHAPTER VI

THE next king came to the throne in 1810, and finding himself unable to cope with the rebellious Moamaria as well as with the continuous strife amongst his chief nobles he proposed to follow the Kocch Raja's recent example and become tributary to the British, but the nobles and people objected to such a procedure. The king (Chandrakant) had in fact written to the Governor-General on the subject, who, however, declined to interfere. The distracted Ahom monarch now turned to Burma for aid, and a force of 6,000 men was despatched from that country in 1816, gathering strength as it journeyed across the Hukong country through being joined by the chiefs of Manipur, Mayangkwan, and Hukong. They reached Nāmrup and were attacked at Ghiladari by an Ahom force under a noble who was in rebellion against the throne. The Burmese, victorious, advanced through eastern Assam, pillaging and laying waste the unhappy country till they reached Jorhat. Here they reinstated Chandrakant and his Prime Minister who had been fugitives; and with the payment of a large war indemnity the Burmese retired over the Patkoi in 1817. Two years of ceaseless petty rebellions and strife followed amongst the nobles, some of whom eventually deposed Chandrakant and set up Purandhar Sing on the throne. Information of this was sent to Burma, a fresh force was sent out from that country, and this time when it reached Assam it had come to stay. A successful engagement against Purandhar Sing's forces led to the Burmese reinstating Chandrakant on the throne, but only as a puppet king, for the entire country soon passed into the actual rule of the invaders, whose commanders scoured the districts, hunting down with merciless severity the adherents of Purandhar who, however, escaped into British territory. The Burmese applied for his extradition, and this was refused. The following year found Chandrakant quarrelling with the Burmese authorities, whose troops, owing to difficulty in supplies, were quartered all over the country, except in the Sadiya district, which they appeared to have left alone to the Hkāmtis and Singphos who had occupied it undisturbed for some years past. Chandrakant deeming this a favourable opportunity for throwing off the yoke of the invaders, got together a force and succeeded in regaining Gauhati. The next two years saw continuous fighting in which sometimes the Burmese and sometimes the Ahoms were successful. Finally the Burmese sent their famous general Māhā Bandula—the commander who in 1825 opposed the British with such vigour at the battle of Donabyu in lower Burma—across with reinforcements, and the Ahoms were utterly defeated in a pitched battle at Mahgarh, losing 1,500 men. Chandrakant fled to Bengal and Bandula sent insolent messages to the English officials saying he would carry the war into their territory if the fugitive was not given up. On this, additional British troops were sent to Goalpāra, Jogighopa, and other frontier outposts ; and all pointed to the coming end of a most intolerable state of affairs in upper Assam.

The Burmese had by now ravaged the land from end to end, a great massacre of the inhabitants of Gauhati took place, life and property were never safe, and the various savage hill tribes utilised the state of confusion existing to harry the plains.

On the 5th of March, 1825, the first Burma war broke out, and Māhā Bandula was recalled to his country to organise forces in lower Burma for repelling the British advance. Orders from Calcutta detailed a force of 3,000 sepoys with guns and an armed flotilla to assemble at Goalpāra under command of Colonel Richards, for the task of turning the Burmese out of the Brahmaputra valley ; and these on the 28th of March occupied Gauhati, the enemy offering little or no resistance. Here in late April Richards was joined by Mr. David Scott, who had marched across the Jaintia hills from Cachar with three companies of the 27th Native Infantry. Desultory fighting took place in the vicinity of Koliabar, to which place Richards advanced, and which ended in his favour. Paucity of supplies here however, constrained the British to return to Gauhati for the rainy season ; and this over, a fresh forward move was made, and the enemy were manœuvred out of Jorhat after several skirmishes. At the end of January, 1826, Richards fought a serious engagement at the Nāmdang river and pushed on to the capital, Rangpur, which was now held in strength by the Burmese. The defences of the city were well arranged, formidable, and mounted many guns. The 57th and 46th Native Infantry attacked with some light field guns, and the right wing of the former corps, leading the attack, being heavily fired on, a number of sepoys fell and a temporary check occurred, until Colonel Richards, with Captain Martin, bringing up the whole of the remainder of the column, the main stockades were escaladed and two masonry temples occupied by the enemy with cannon were captured with considerable loss in wounded to the British troops, amongst whom were Colonel Richards and Lieutenant Brooke. This action dispirited the Burmese, whose forces breaking up, a large number were pursued and driven into the hills, while many threw down their arms and settled quietly in Assam. In June this year, the Burmese who had retreated across the Patkoi range, finding the Singphos ready to join them, returned and made a last effort against Sadiya, but were worsted in an encounter at Bisa by Captain Neufville with a wing of the 57th Native Infantry, whose success was the means of liberating some 6,000 Assamese captives. Between the Burmese and Singphos, in the past five years it is stated that upwards of 30,000 Assamese had been enslaved and taken out of the country.

The Brahmaputra and the Surma valleys (Cachar) had now been entirely cleared of the Burmese forces, who were also ejected from Manipur by Raja Gambhir Sing, and the unfortunate country now came permanently under British rule, depopulated, starving, and in the greatest misery. A writer on this country in 1873, Mr. T. T. Cooper, remarks that "of all countries bordering on India which have come into British possession, there is none whose history is so mournful as Assam, none wherein the mistaken policy of the Indián Government in the last century is recorded in more painful evidences. Had we maintained a protectorate when Welsh restored order, the country might have been saved."

With the expulsion of the Burmese the English began to take up the difficult task of administering the country, rendered all the more difficult as the Burmese had removed old landmarks, and the people were by now a mass of conflicting parties. Mr. David Scott was at once appointed Agent to the Governor-General of all the country up to the Sadiya and Matak districts, near the present Dibrughar, in the extreme east, with Colonel Cooper and Captains Neufville and White to assist him. A corps raised originally for service in Cuttack was transferred now to Assam to strengthen the hands of these officers. It became the Assam Light Infantry, and was quartered first at Rangpur, and later at Gauhati. The Chief of Matak (Moran) having shown considerable ability, was left in charge of his own district on his agreeing to pay tribute and to provide a certain number of troops on occasion arising, and this continued till 1842. Sadiya, which had been overrun by the Hkāmtis gradually since 1794, was left to the jurisdiction of a man known as the Sadiya Khowa Gohain, who agreed to furnish a force of armed and drilled soldiers as a protection for the border. In 1833, owing to immense extent of country now in English hands which was not easy to administer, it was decided to make over the portion from the Dhansiri to the Dibru river to Purandhar Sing, who was consequently reinstated; while Mr. David Scott, as first Commissioner of Assam, administered the entire country from the Dhansiri river to the confines of Bengal. The Assam Light Infantry and certain Sebundy Corps (local levies) were distributed at prominent centres throughout the land, a strong detachment being at Jorhat, Purandhar's capital, and another at Sadiya under Colonel White, the Political Agent to the Hkāmtis and Singphos. In 1835 disputes arose between the Khowa Gohain and the chief of Matak over land, which caused friction; and this together with the stoppage of slave trading and a fear of being taxed, produced a state of discontent which burst into rebellion in January, 1839. Colonel White, placing too much confidence on the illusive permanence of Hkāmti allegiance, was unprepared, and even had no guard over his own house though warned of trouble, which came on the night of the 28th of January. At 2 a.m. four large bodies of Hkāmtis, with a few Singphos, suddenly attacked Sadiya at different points, firing the houses and resolutely attacking the main stockade. In a moment all was confusion and uproar, the enemy using swords and spears to great effect. Colonel White was killed while leaving his house to join the troops, pierced by nine spear wounds, and eighty odd men, women and children were cut up before the officers got their men together in groups, when discipline at last prevailed, the stockade was retaken and the enemy pursued out of the place. Next day several villages in the district were attacked and destroyed by the Hkāmtis, more troops were hurried up from Jorhat, and the country was now entirely taken over by the Government. The Hkāmti element was largely deported far down country, where eventually they settled and became good agriculturists. By 1840 English residences, church, etc., were springing up in Gauhati, which had become the headquarter station of the new Assam Government. The entire country, having now come under British rule, it only remains to touch upon a few industrial points of interest before moving on to an account of the border tribes and expeditions. The great industry for which Assam is noted is that of tea, which about 1823 was first discovered as an indigenous plant in the surrounding hills by a Mr. R. Bruce, at that time British agent to the Ahom king, Chandrakant. But the matter was not taken up until ten years later, when Mr. Bruce's brother started the first tea plantation near the mouth of the Kundil river, above Sadiya. In 1839 the Assam Tea Company was formed, and began opening gardens at Jaipur, Dibrughar, and on the Tingri river. Thence onward the tea industry flourished throughout the country. In spite of the great raised roadways, which history shows us had been constructed in different parts of the country, its communications generally were exceedingly bad, which state, in spite of our having made two so-called Trunk Roads both north and south of the Brahmaputra in 1854, may be said to exist still. In 1847 the first steamer service succeeded the laborious and slow boat journey, but for many years they only plied as far as Gauhati. It was between 1838 and 1840 that a decision was arrived at to locate the chief military station in upper Assam at Dibrughar, the necessity for having a garrison nearer to the Hkāmtis and Singphos having been shown by disturbances during the past few years. Captain Vetch, afterwards General Hamilton Vetch, the British officer controlling the Matak (Moran) country in which Dibrughar lies, selected the site; and lines, fort, jail, and other building rapidly followed. The church, built by the late General Reid (R.E.) is a memorial to Colonel White, who, we have seen before, was killed at Sadiya. It was not, however, until about 1880 that a regular steamer service plied up and down the Brahmaputra, and that this far eastern station was thus connected up with Bengal. Towards the end of the "thirties" coal was found, first on the Safrai river where it emerges from the hills, a little east of Sibsagor; and a Commission was formed to discover if it was workable, and to what extent, in these hills. More being found in the Tipam hills, and the Commission reporting favourably, Mr. Landers, Special Assistant to the Commissioner, in 1842 opened and worked the first mine on the Nāmsangia range in the Dikkoo valley, after which other mines beyond Dibrughar were opened, and the industry has since progressed with enormous strides. This, together with the tea industry in the Dibrughar district and the difficulty of transporting both commodities to the river steamers, led in 1878 to the first idea of railway construction, which was favoured by Sir Stewart Bayley. The following year a company was formed, but owing to difficulties in raising money for the project, no advance was made till 1881 when, after a committee had thoroughly reported on the Mākum coal fields and oil wells, showing the high value of the same, money was raised in London to the amount of £600,000, and the work put in hand on New Year's day, 1882. On the 1st of May following the first engine was plying over the section near Dibrughar, and by the end of the year twenty miles were open to traffic. During this time work was also progressing from Mākum at the other end of the line, as material could be floated up to that point along the Dihing river; and on Christmas Day, 1883, the rails were joined and through communication with Dibrughar was established. Railhead was then named Margherita, in honour of the Queen of Italy, due to the fact that the Chevalier R. Paganini, an Italian, was chief engineer of that rail section. A year or two later a branch line was opened from Talup to Saikwa Ghat, opposite Sadiya, our furthest frontier post. An interesting feature of these coal-fields, particularly that of Ledo six miles from Margherita, is the number of isolated hills of pure coal standing above the ground surface, which obviates the labour of deep mining. Following on this successful railway enterprise came two light lines at Jorhat and Tezpur, and these again were followed by the Assam Bengal Railway which now connects the port of Chittagong with Dibrughar, a length of some 600 miles, with a branch line from Lumding Junction to Gauhati of 150 miles. The first surveys of this great undertaking began about 1894, and work started two years later at different points along the route. Immense difficulties were experienced by the engineers in carrying the line through the North Cachar hills and the great Nambhor forest, which sections cost fabulous sums of money and are monuments of engineering skill. In 1899 ballast trains were running over portions of the line, which was not open throughout for traffic till 1902 owing to delays caused by the immense difficulties to be overcome in the hills section. With the start of this line came the hope to link up Burma with upper Assam by carrying a line from Dibrughar through the Hukong valley to Mogoung on the Upper Burma Railway system, and a survey party with escort crossed the Patkoi in 1896, while another party surveyed an alternative route to Burma, which was to take off at Lumding and follow a line viâ Berrima, in the Kaccha Naga hills, to the Mayankhong valley, and so to Manipur. Both projects, however, were temporarily shelved; the Manipur one because of the expense, as the tunnelling and difficulties in crossing the stupendous gorges of the upper Barak river would have been prohibitive in cost. Now that deeper interest has been stirred in North Eastern Frontier matters, these two projects are once again coming to the front, and the Hukong valley route is generally stated to be the most practicable from commercial and engineering points of view.

CHAPTER VII

RELIGIONS OF THE EARLY ASSAMESE AND NOTABLE REMAINS

THE subject of religion is a somewhat difficult one to trace correctly. From old legends it would appear the earliest religion of the aborigines, namely the Kachāris, with whom are allied the Kocch, Chutiya and Morān (Matak) peoples, was animism and a worship of demons, etc. When Hinduism was introduced is uncertain, but it undoubtedly was in vogue about 830 A.D., in the reign of one Hajāra. Hannay is of opinion that Kāmarupa was one of the earliest conquests of the Indian Khettri kings about 400 B.C., and was then the seat of that primitive form of Hinduism, or perhaps Buddhism, which existed previous to the introduction of Brahminical Hinduism about the middle of the fifteenth century, brought in by certain Brahmins from the city of Gaur in Bengal. This took a great hold on the country, even the Tai (Ahom) conquerors coming over to it in the early part of the seventeenth century. That Buddhism was introduced is certain, but it is equally certain it took no very lasting hold on the people and it was only of comparatively short duration.

Many of the old Hindu temples have been built on and with the remains of what once were Buddhist shrines. At Hājo, once an important centre of

Closer View of Individual Stone, Dimāpur.

Moghul rule, and opposite Gauhati, six or seven miles from the river, on a wooded hill 300 feet high, stands a remarkable and celebrated temple containing a large image of Buddha six feet high and cut from a solid block of black stone. The figure is in what is known as the " contemplative attitude," and is annually visited still by thousands of both Hindus and Buddhists from all parts of India. This temple is endowed with lands, dancing girls, and beneficed priests ; as are also the celebrated Kāmakhya temples, which are said to have taken the place of ancient Buddhist shrines.

Thibetans and Bhootanese believe that Buddha died in Kāmarupa, while the learned Hungarian traveller, Csomo de Kōros claims that the Saint died in Gauhati " under a pair of Sal trees." The great Chinese traveller Huien Tsiang, had also the same idea ; but he records in the early part of the seventh century that, though the people adored the Devas, there seemed to be little faith in the Saint himself, and that no places in which Buddhist priests could assemble appeared to exist. Such disciples as there are, he says, are certainly of a pure faith, but pray more or less secretly. Buddha lived in the sixth century B.C., and on his death, which some assert occurred at Kusināgra in upper Bengal, and others in Assam at Gauhati, the first Buddhist synod was held at Rajagriha in Bengal, the second being held a hundred years later, or about the early part of 400 B.C., in Wesāli Löng—the Buddhist name for Assam ; which goes to prove that this religion must in those far off days have had a certain amount of hold on the country reaching as far as the Sadiya district, where Major Hannay states are to be found ruins of temples of undoubted Buddhist origin. The religion deteriorated in the succeeding centuries until it reached the condition in which Huien Tsiang found it.

In the centuries preceding his travels in this part of Asia waves of Buddhism had passed further east from India, and by way of Thibet, Assam, and the Arrakan coast, had spread itself far afield. But it is not till as late as 1016 A.D. that we find the gentle teaching of Buddha introduced throughout Burma as the State religion by Anarawthaza, the great conqueror and religious reformer. It developed in course of time into the puritan school (Hinayāna) or Southern

THE BIG TANK AND RESTHOUSE AT DIMĀPUR EXCAVATED HUNDREDS OF YEARS AGO BY THE KACHĀRIS.

Buddhism, spreading to Siam and Ceylon; as opposed to the Northern Buddhism (Mahāyāna) or debased ritualistic school embraced by China, Mongolia, Corea, Thibet, and Nepal.

Hinduism, known in Assam for centuries alongside of Buddhism, began extending itself more thoroughly throughout the land about the ninth century, but gradually assumed a debased style due to the Trantric form of Hinduism, also known as Sakta Hinduism, which in its main idea is the worship of the female principle, typifying creative power. The worship was accompanied by human sacrifices and orgies beyond description in honour of Kāmakhya, goddess of desire, and an incarnation of the dread goddess Kali. Hamilton, writing of this country in 1839, says: "Assam is likened in old times to a sort of Paphian land, the seat of promiscuous pleasures, loose manners, and mystery, due to the rise of the Tantric form of Hinduism which the Brahmins inculcated in these wild parts and which enabled them through the worship of Kāmakhya to share in sensual gratifications from which otherwise they would have been excluded." The ancient temples on the Nilachal hill, near Gauhati, formed the centre of this worship, but many others exist as far afield as the Tāmasāri Mai and the Bhora Bhoori temples at the foot of the Mishmi hills not far east of Sadiya. At all these shrines human beings were offered up as sacrifices. Colonel Dalton has given an account of these sacrifices, which obtained almost up to the British occupation of Assam, by certain Deori Chutiya priests of the Tāmasāri Mai. These described how the victim was detained some time at the temple, being fed until deemed sufficiently fat to please the flesh-eating Goddess. On the appointed day he was led forth in magnificent clothes to be shown to the crowds assembled for the hideous ceremony. He was then led by a private path trodden only by the priests to a deep pit at the back of the temple. Here his gay raiment was stripped off and he was decapitated, the body falling into the pit, the head being added to the heap of ghastly skulls piled in front of the shrine.

In the early part of 1500 A.D. a Hindu reformer arose, named Shankar Deb, a Kayasth of Nowgong, who preached a purer Hinduism based on prayer rather than on sacrifices; but being much persecuted by the Brahmins of Gauhati he went into the Kocch country, where his ideas and new faith obtained a better hearing. In course of time, this religion gaining a strong footing in Kāmarupa, spread further, until in the seventeenth century we see Gadardhar Sing persecuting its adherents, as they had by then become a formidable power in the land. A hundred years later Sakta Hinduism was firmly established as the State religion, and soon came into conflict with the Vishnubite followers of Shankar Deb, leading up to the sect of the Moamaria, and a series of religious rebellions which plunged the country into the deepest misery, and from which it was only relieved by the advent of British rule. The Moamaria were a sect of the purer Vishnubite faith, differing only from what Shankar Deb inculcated in that they paid more distinction to caste matters, and were not so averse to sacrifices and idol worship. The Assamese of the present day are Hindus, but they are lax in religious rites, and their ceremonies are often very different from those practised in India.

Notable Remains.

Of all the ruins in Assam that have excited the interest of archæological savants, the old fort at Dimāpur in the Nambhor forest stands pre-eminently first; not so much from the fort itself as from the remarkable carved stone monoliths which stand within its area. Dimāpur, as we have seen, was up to the middle of the sixteenth century the capital of the Kachāri people; and evidences of sites, causeways, etc., cut

CLOSER VIEW OF INDIVIDUAL STONES, DIMĀPUR.

through by the Assam and Bengal Railway, show it to have been of very considerable extent, the present old fort having been a sort of citadel. It is a square; each face six to seven hundred yards long had originally a gateway, except the one overlooking the

Dhansiri river. Of these, only one on the east face now remains in a fair state of preservation. The brick walls are all thrown down but easily traceable, as are also several tanks inside. It was first noticed by Lieutenant Biggs, who in 1841 made a tour from Nowgong to the Naga hills and opened a salt depot at Dimāpur, which was then on the border of British territory; but it remained hidden in its dense covering of forest growth till about 1892, when a

THE REMARKABLE CARVED STONES AS DISCOVERED IN THE OLD KACHĀRI FORT AT DIMĀPUR.

small portion inside was cleared. This revealed the remarkable collection of monoliths standing inside, or rather some still erect, others thrown down and cracked by earthquakes. What these represent, and by what people carved and set up, has baffled many a savant. Ferguson says that they are unique of their kind in Asia, and were obviously there long before the fort, set up by a race long forgotten, but still venerated in the mystery surrounding them, by the Kachāris. They stand, enormous blocks of sandstone in four rows six yards apart, sixteen in each row, those at the ends being ten to twelve feet, the centre four being fifteen to seventeen feet high. The two rows to the east are shaped not unlike gigantic "lingam" stones, the two western ones taking the shape of a V, and are said to be evidences of Phallic worship. The tops of the latter have deep slots cut into them, pointing to their having possibly supported a roof; but whether the roof of a temple or of a covered way to a temple long since crumbled away, it is impossible to say. All the stones are elaborately carved with representations of birds, animals, spear heads, and this must have been done after the stones were set up, as the nearest places from which the stone could have been quarried are some ten miles off in the gorge near Nichuguard, and the carving would have been badly damaged in transit. In Lord Curzon's time, whose interest for ancient remains is well known, these fallen and cracked monoliths have been set up in their places, the broken pieces secured with iron bands, and the surrounding ground completely cleared and fenced in for their preservation. Further clearing inside the fort has revealed a smaller set of similar stones less elaborately carved, and one solitary giant stone some twenty feet high. In the vicinity of Dimāpur are two enormous and deep tanks, one being over 300 yards on each face, with high banks, on one of which, up to 1901, stood the old rest-house looking over the fine sheet of water away to the Naga hills. It is said that ten other tanks are known of in this locality, all dating from the early Kachāri days. At

Jāmaguri, thirty odd miles north-east of Dimāpur, near the Doyang river, are the remains of another ancient city with similar monoliths, but this has not been properly explored yet; while at Deopāni, in the neighbourhood of Borpathar, stands a single gigantic monolith carved as are those at Dimāpur which was discovered by a civil engineer when con-

THE CARVED STONES IN DIMĀPUR FORT RESTORED AND SET UP, AS AT PRESENT.

structing the cart road from Golaghat to Dimāpur after the Manipur rising of 1891, and while searching in the forest for stone for bridging purposes. At Maibong, a small station on the Assam and Bengal Railway, are to be seen distinct traces of massive brick walls which surrounded the second Kachāri capital, and which are now covered with forest and jungle. Carved stones, stone images, portions of stones with inscriptions cut into them, fragments of pillars, excavated tanks, etc., are frequently found by coolies and herdsmen and brought to those interested in such things, and many of the best have found their way into museums. The most complete of these remains as yet discovered here lies a mile from the station down the Mahur river, and is a gigantic boulder eighteen to twenty feet high and over ninety feet round at the base, the upper half of which

Ancient and Remarkable Temple Carved from a Huge Boulder at Maibong.

is carved into the shape of a temple with doors, projecting eaves, some rough ornamentation, and an inscription carved on the west side, gives a date, namely, 1683 Hindu era, representing 1721 of ours. The temple is apparently solid and is not used; nor, as the writer was told, does it appear to have any sanctity left, for it is never visited by "fakirs" and such like who annually make their "tirith," or pilgrimages, to ancient shrines in Assam. Maibong lies in a charmingly wooded valley watered by the Mahur river, which in its lower reaches holds good fishing, and is overlooked by the Mahadeo mountain rising to some 5000 feet.

The ruins of Garhgaon have been mentioned in the history, so we pass on to the far eastern corner of Assam on the borderland of the Mishmis and Abors, to where stand the remains of the once large and flourishing cities of Kūndina and Prithiminagar, and certain famous temples. And here, as the writer has never had the opportunity of reaching this locality himself, Major Hannay's account of these in his article to the Journal of the Asiatic Society Bengal, 1848, will serve us the better, as he fancies no one else has taken the trouble to explore those regions, though many of our frontier expeditions of late years have passed them closely by. Kūndina (Kūndilpur), which Hannay and party visited, is a hill fort at the foot of the mountains between the Dikrang and Dibong rivers, some sixteen miles north of Sadiya. The path led six miles across the plain and thence up the bed of the Dikrang. On reaching the hill the only track found was that beaten down by wild elephants, and frequently paths had to be cut for several hours; after which they reached a fine piece of table-land covered with splendid timber trees. Here they came upon the first traces of a bygone people in a high earth rampart facing the plains. A little further on was found the remains of a strong parapet, the lower portion of which was of solid hewn granite blocks topped by a wall of well-made bricks about five feet high, apparently loop-holed for spears and arrows. There were signs of gateways and many cross walls, but all had crumbled into the heaps of bricks which littered the locality. From what they saw, these defences surrounded an immense area, while in the Dikrang valley were seen numerous debris of earthen vessels totally different in shape from those used by the Assamese, and which they found closely resembled the earthenware of Gangetic India.

Hannay records that all the remains are of great age and originally were substantially built of good stone and bricks. Cement was unknown then, and certain rectangular turns in the walls pointed to a knowledge of flank defence.

The party spent a week on the Dikrang river exploring the site of another ancient city spoken of as Prithiminagar, where they found an eighteen-foot high earth rampart with ditch circling round for several miles north and north-west. Inside this rampart, now supporting enormous forest trees, they found several very large tanks, one measuring 280 by ninety yards, with ruined bathing ghats of hewn sandstone. A brick gateway was found, and a raised road leading to the river, where large stone slabs lying about suggested the remains of a bridge. This must have enclosed the site of a very large town. Both these places, he conjectures, were built by one people, the masonry and bricks being of one pattern, But who were these people ? And when and wherefrom did the wild Abors and Mishmis come who now hold these hills ? Popular tradition, Hannay says, as well as local evidences, go to show that the Brahmaputra in the far-off past ran much closer to the mountains than it does now, which would have brought the river close to these ancient cities. The little river Kūndil gave its name to one of the towns, namely Kūndilpur, also known as Kūndina and as Bishmaknagar, from the name of its legendary founder; and where the stream joins the Brahmaputra, namely

CARVED STONES DUG UP AT MAIBONG.

at Kūndilmukh, was located for many years a British military outpost.

Another visit of exploration was paid by Hannay to the famous shrine of Tāmasāri Mai or the Copper Temple, and to that of Bhora Bhoori in the same locality, namely in the Sadiya district. Of the former, he writes that this sacred spot, eight miles north-east of Chunpūra (Sonpura), which lies ten miles east of Kūndilmukh, now covered with dense forest, stands on a little stream, the Dalpāni. In ancient times this shrine and the once populous lands around were undoubtedly connected with the western end of Assam by the stupendous raised roadway from Kamātāpur (Cooch Behar) through Narainpur to the extreme east of Assam, and also presumably to the cities just alluded to, long stretches of which are still in use. Several generations have now passed away since the votaries of these temples were numerous enough to keep the roads leading to them open. The Tāmasāri Mai was dedicated to Kāmakhya and the Yoni; but Shiva and the Lingam were also worshipped with all barbarous rites, including human sacrifices, which latter obtained it is known in the early part of the nineteenth century. In 1850 Hannay knew of certain families living near Sadiya who for generations past had been specially set aside to provide the doubtful honour of becoming victims to the dread Goddess. He gives a detailed description of the size and shape of this temple, speaks of the well-hewn blocks of granite of which it is built, and from the fact that in one part he finds a thin layer of mortar between the bricks composing the upper part, he assumes the ancient shrine to have been rebuilt about the time of the Brahminical revival, namely, about the middle of the fifteenth century. The doorway appears to have been elaborately carved, and in front stood an elephant carved out of a huge block of porphyritic granite of a hardness which must have required well-tempered tools to work with. Tradition says the tusks, no longer existent, were of silver. The whole is surrounded by a brick terrace which is ornamented with tiles let in, having stamped upon them in high relief, figures of Hindu Avatars. Very little remained then of the copper roofing. The Bhora Bhoori temple Hannay and party also found their way to, which lies ten miles from Sadiya, the last four miles being up the bed of the Dikrang river

"MURTA," OR IDOL, FOUND AT MAIBONG.

till a small stream, the Deopāni, was reached. Here they came on what is generally stated to be the most ancient as well as the most sacred spot in Assam. Orthodox Hindus consider it a shrine to Mahadeo, but Hannay is certain of its Buddhist origin. There is a large hexagonal altar in a well-flagged courtyard surrounded by a rampart of hewn sandstone blocks, the inner side of which is faced with bricks. In front of this altar is a stone terrace on which offerings were placed, and about sixty paces from the altar is the second rampart and deep ditch outside. There were no signs of gateways, but a raised roadway led out from the west face of the altar. There are also traces of this altar having had a roof over it once, but this has long since vanished. Both sacred spots are in an absolutely ruinous state and overgrown with jungle round and upon them. This growth of course gradually displaces stones, and the general dilapidation is probably increased by the numerous wild elephants tearing down the shrubs from the highest points reachable, and rubbing themselves against the walls.

In the vicinity of Sibsagor, at Garhgaon, and Rangpur, are still to be seen remains of old Ahom forts, the palace, several large tanks, and some fine Hindu temples. Charaideo, the first capital of note, and for long a place of sanctity for Ahom kings, has little or nothing left visible of its former glory beyond a temple, a tank, and the mounds covering the burial places of certain kings. In the centre of the Dihing Company's tea plantation stands a large ancient temple with a splendid avenue of Nahor trees of great age leading up to it; this was discovered when the ground for plantation was being cleared of its dense forests. In this neighbourhood, when out shooting in the jungles, one frequently comes across evidence of the sites of towns and villages, artificial irrigation channels, tanks, and groves of fine old mango and jack fruit trees, marking where once gardens had stood. This in the heart of the forest—unmistakable signs of a former thriving population in what was till recent years perhaps one of the wildest districts of eastern Assam.

While on this subject a reference may well be made here to the worship of stones by the Khasias and certain of the Naga tribes. These are set up to

INSCRIBED STONES DUG UP AT MAIBONG.

commemorate deaths, raids, hunting successes, and village incidents of importance. Some are set up, as amongst certain hill tribes in Manipur, in the name of a deity, but are not objects actually connected with religious ideas. The tribe whose monoliths reach an enormous size and are arranged in avenues on the way up to their villages is that of Marām, a Naga community occupying the hill country about the upper Barak waters and eastern slopes of the Barail range, not far from the Naga hills boundary. These people have erected immense stones for centuries past, arranging them in symmetrical rows, avenues, circles, and singly. Two huge monoliths in the village of Marām are venerated as the deity presiding over hunting matters. The labour of dragging these huge and heavy stones up hill sides is very great, the stones being levered on to a stout timber sledge and then dragged by bands

THE REMARKABLE "STONEHENGE" AT TOGWEMA, NAGA HILLS.

of men using ropes of stout creepers till the spot for erection is reached, when it is again levered off the sledge into a hole and then lifted up until completely erect, the process sometimes covering days and weeks. The most remarkable of these "Stonehenges" is to be seen at the village of Togwema (or Uilong), a few miles west of Marām, and which has only been up to date visited by three Englishmen, including the writer. Here on a spur just outside the village, now of no great size, stands thirty-two monoliths arranged in a large oval, from which again start lines of fourteen monoliths, the height of all varying between eight feet and thirteen and a half feet, and the breadth between two feet and nine and a half feet. The thickness of each is generally about two feet. In the oval of stones it is customary for the young men of the place to hold their dances and wrestling bouts, which occur on the annual festival of the dead. These stones, the writer was told, were very many centuries old, and were put up when Togwema village was a large and powerful one, which has since many generations gradually declined in strength and importance. The erection of this "Stonehenge" would be quite impossible in the present day. From popular traditions and from actual practices in the present day with stones of lesser size, it is possible to obtain some idea of the expenditure in energy, and the resources of the people of the past required for such stupendous undertakings.

CHAPTER VIII

BHOOTAN

Having now dealt with the history of Assam and the reasons leading to its coming into our hands, we can now deal with the different interesting border tribes and their countries, commencing from the west, namely, with the Bhootanese, a Thibeto-Burman race dwelling east of Darjiling and north of the Cooch Behar border.

The Bhootan hills, as they are alluded to, and which border Assam to the north-west, are about 220 miles long by ninety or so in breadth, and they separate Thibet from the Brahmaputra valley. Very little is known of this country, which was first visited in 1774 and 1783 by Bogle and Captain Turner respectively, who, on commercial trips to Thibet, made their routes through Bhootan. The next to penetrate these hills was Captain Pemberton in 1838, who describes the people as "in disposition excellent, they possess an equanimity of temper almost bordering on apathy and are indolent to an extreme degree. They are also illiterate, immoral, and victims of the most unqualified superstition." In describing the officials, he says: "the highest officers of state in Bhootan are shameless beggars and liars of the first magnitude, whose most solemn pledged words are violated without the slightest hesitation. They play bully and sycophant with equal readiness, exhibiting in their conduct a rare compound of official pride and presumption, together with the low cunning of needy mediocrity." Mr. Claude White, however, expresses himself on them in more favourable terms since his visit to their country in 1905.

The people are professed Buddhists, though still propitiating evil spirits; polyandry is the prevailing domestic custom and the habits of all classes are filthy to a degree. The men are strongly built, with athletic figures, of dark complexions, and unpleasantly heavy and cunning faces.

With a people possessing these unamiable characteristics we had but little to do until well into the middle of last century, when we came into unpleasant contact with them, due to their continual acts of aggression along the borders of the Dooars or large tracts of low hills and terai land lying between the Himalayas and the Assam plains. In 1792, when Welsh's expedition entered Assam, it was found the Bhootanese were exercising authority as far into the plains as Kāmāli Alli, though for how long this had been going on is not known; presumably the weak government of Gaurinath's reign had favoured the extension of Bhootanese land grabbing. However, this condition could not be put up with when the British began to administer Assam in 1832, and Mr. David Scott ordered them back into the Dooars. These, the Assam Dooars, ten years later were appropriated by the Government in punishment for various acts of aggression and plunder. As these Dooars had formerly belonged rightly to the Assamese kings, and, owing to the arbitrary severity of the Bhootan rulers had almost been depopulated, this act of the

THE HUNTING STONES AT MARĀM.

British Commissioners cannot be viewed as a harsh proceeding. These tracts now came under our rule and formed part of the present districts of Kāmrup and Darrang; but one of the eastern Dooars, that of Kalling, for some time was subject to a curious dual control, the reason of which was not apparent, namely, that for eight months in the year the inhabitants belonged to the Tongsa Penlo subject to the Dharm and Deb Rajas of Bhootan, and during the remaining four months (June 15 to October 15) the people reverted to British jurisdiction. In 1842 this anomalous condition ceased to exist. Of the two rulers just mentioned it may be said the Dharm Raja is the spiritual, while the Deb Raja is the temporal head of Bhootan.

By 1845 the most easterly of the Dooars had been brought under our rule, and now Government decided that a sum of money, 10,000 rupees, should be paid annually to the two Rajas as some compensation for the loss of revenue entailed by them on our taking over the land.

In 1852 a misunderstanding arose between the British and Thibetan Governments concerning the Raja of Gelong in the hills overlooking the most easterly of the Assam Dooars. This Raja, having been set in authority over other petty chiefs by the Thibetan Government, took advantage of this little show of power to declare himself independent. Troops from Lhassa were sent against him, and after some stubborn fighting the Gelong Raja was driven across our border, and his extradition demanded in most peremptory terms. This was followed up by an army being pushed down towards the plains, and at one time a Thibetan invasion of Assam appeared imminent. However, a small British force of 400 sepoys and two guns being hurried up to the Darrang border, further Thibetan intentions were checked without actual hostility. A treaty was then signed by the Thibetans by which they agreed to our terms, and the hostile force returned to Lhassa. Though these measures gave peace to the Assam Dooars, those abutting on the province of Bengal were still frequently subjected to plunder and outrages. In spite of remonstrances from Government, which only

A SOLITARY MONOLITH.

elicited insolent replies, things went on in this unsatisfactory way until 1860 when, as a punishment, the estate of Fallacotta was annexed by the British, and a native mission was sent to explain the situation and intentions of Government to the Deb and Dharm Rajas of Bhootan. This producing no effect, Mr.

Eden (Secretary to the Bengal Government) was sent in 1863 to Ponāka, their capital, to make a final effort towards better relations between the two Governments. Eden, however, on arrival at Ponāka was received with contumely by the Bhootan court and practically held a prisoner; until only by signing a treaty under protest, which was perfectly unworkable, would the Durbar guarantee him and his party a safe conduct out of their country. The patience of the British Government being now exhausted, war became unavoidable. The Bhootanese forces were said to number 10,000 men armed with matchlocks, bows and arrows, and short heavy swords. Their matchlocks, though clumsy, were effective at 400 yards; while a case occurred at Dewangiri of one of our men being shot at 800 yards by one of these weapons. But the bow is their favourite arm with which they constantly practise and are very expert. They were this time found to act well on the defence and were good at field works. That they are not devoid of courage is shown by what occurred at Dewangiri in 1865, when they defeated and put to rout a British force of 800 sepoys and ten British officers; and again near the same place the defence of a stockade by 150 Bhootanese, who fought it out to the bitter end, excited admiration.

A picturesque feature in their country are the old mediaeval forts built to control the trade route from Thibet and to guard against invasion on that side. These are well described by Mr. C. White in the report of his visit in 1905, and it would be interesting to know how this people got to know of the pattern of such defensive structures unlike what are found in the parts of India adjacent to their country, and far more resembling some old-time European castle.

Active measures having now been decided on against Bhootan, a force in four columns was assembled to enter the country and exact reparation for insults to our envoy, property raided, captives carried off, and general aggressiveness of the past few years.

The Dewangiri column was the principal one, and consisted of the 43rd Assam L.I. (now 7th

METHOD OF DRAGGING THESE STONES ON SLEDGES TO THEIR FINAL RESTING PLACE.

Goorkha Rifles) one and a half companies Sappers, one squadron 5th B.C., and two mountain guns, with a wing of the 12th B.I. and Assam local Artillery in reserve at Gauhati.

The Sidli column of one squadron of 5th B.C. and two squadrons 14th B.C., a wing of the 44th Assam Light Infantry (now the 8th Goorkha Rifles), one and a half companies Sappers, and three mountain guns, was to operate in the hills between the Sankōsh and Manās rivers

The Buxa column a wing of the 11th B.I., one squadron 14th B.C., and three mountain guns was to operate west of the Sankōsh river beyond the northern border of Cooch Behar.

The Dāling column based on Jalpaigori consisted of a wing of the 11th B.I., two squadrons 5th B.C., one company Sappers, with two mountain guns and two mortars was to move on Dāling fort between the Jaldaka and Tista rivers.

The 80th Foot was held in readiness at Darjiling.

In the end of November all was in readiness and the Dāling column opened proceedings by moving first. On the 5th of December, 1864, the force reached Dāling, which was attacked and shelled next day. A breach being effected, the place was assaulted, the enemy evacuating it before our troops got in. The defence for a time was well conducted, for our losses were three British officers and seven men killed, seven officers and fifty-seven men wounded; while though our fire on the fort had been heavy for eight hours, only four dead were found in it. Four days later the fort of Dumsong was taken, and the troops moving further east reached Chumarchi fort, which was captured on the 2nd of January, 1865, with a loss to us of two killed and fifteen wounded.

While this was going on the Buxa column had occupied Buxa without opposition, and left a garrison to hold it, while the rest scoured the country.

The Sidli and Dewangiri columns working in concert viâ Bhijnì and Kurramkotta, or Kumrikotta, captured Dewangiri on the 12th of December with the loss of only one man.

A garrison of six companies 43rd Assam Light

Infantry and two guns was left here, while the rest of the force moved west to establish a post at Bishensing. Early in February, it being thought operations were at an end, the columns, excepting these garrisons, were withdrawn to the plains. The Bhootanese however, were not done with, for in early February, 1865, they re-assembled and began attacking the garrisons left behind. At Dewangiri they succeeded one morning early in entering the camp quietly, and

AVENUE OF MONOLITHS NEAR MARĀM.

suddenly cutting the tent ropes, all was soon in confusion, and hand-to-hand conflicts followed when the enemy were at length beaten off, having inflicted a loss to the garrison of one British officer and four men killed, one British officer and thirty-one men wounded. For three days the garrison were surrounded and its water supply cut off. On the 4th of February they were compelled to retreat, which was commenced the following day under disastrous circumstances. The way was lost, the

Bhootanese, 1,500 strong, followed closely, a panic set in, many wounded were left behind, and the two guns fell into the enemy's hands. The force, completely disorganised, at last reached the plains. Determined attacks were also made on the Chumarchi, Balla, and Buxa stockades, and were not beaten off without considerable losses to us. At Buxa the garrison was obliged to retire with two officers and thirteen men wounded.

Immediate steps were taken to send up reinforcements, and the 55th and the 80th Foot, 19th, 29th, and 31st Punjabi Infantry with two batteries of Artillery were ordered up to Assam under command of General Tombs. Two columns were formed: the right to concentrate at Gauhati and to advance on Dewangiri, the left from Jalpaigori to move into the western hills on Buxa and Dāling. After a series of minor skirmishes Dewangiri was captured after a stiff fight, with a loss to us of four officers and thirty-five men wounded; the fort and defences were then demolished. The left column encountered severe opposition at Balla, losing three killed and one officer and nineteen men wounded in the capture of a strong Bhootanese stockade, which the enemy held to the last in hand-to-hand conflict with detachments of the 18th and 19th P.I. The operations were brought to a close in early April, 1865, and with Dāling and Buxa garrisoned in strength the force returned to Assam. The Bhootan Durbar, however, did not yet come to terms, nor had they given up the captured guns; it was therefore found desirable to again enter their hills and advance to the capital Ponāka. To this end a force of two wings of British infantry and six battalions of Native Infantry were put in motion, and after one action at Salika on the 6th of February, 1866, the Bhootanese finally submitted. The guns were given up and a treaty signed by the Deb and Dharm Rajas agreeing to all our terms, which included the final annexation of the Bengal Dooars and the cessation of all revenue hitherto received by Bhootan for the Assam Dooars. The end of this war saw the Bhootan Durbar finally deprived for good and all of the Dooars and lands they had held below the hills, and the allowances hitherto paid to the Durbar on account of the Assam Dooars and Fallacotta were, of course, stopped. Later, however, Government reconsidered the matter of allowances on its being known that the Bhootan aristocracy drew all their revenue from these plains' lands. It was rightly surmised that entire deprivation of such revenues would only produce a discontented, turbulent set of neighbours along our border; so in spite of all provocation the British Government arranged that a sum of Rs. 25,000, in which the Assam Dooars' allowance was merged, should be paid annually, and the boundary line from the Manās river on the west to the Deosham river on the east was definitely laid down, and a military post established in the hills at Buxa; after which our frontier relations with these people became extremely simple. With regard to direct trade between Assam and Thibet which formerly existed, Hamilton states that Lhassa used to send an annual caravan of silver and rock salt to a place called "Chouna," two months' march from the capital, where for long a mart had been established close to the border of both countries, and that four miles from Chouna on the Assam side a similar mart existed at "Gegunshar," to which place rice, silk, iron, and lac were brought for exchange. These two places, however, are not shown on any maps, and in the early part of last century the trade appears to have ceased, to be revived again by a Lieutenant Rutherford in 1833 at Udalgūri, in Darrang district, which still continues and is visited annually by crowds of interesting peoples from Bhootan, Thibet, and even China. Another trade route between Thibet, Bhootan, and Assam, passes through Tawang to Udalgūri, and is in constant use.

CHAPTER IX

AKAS

The tribe next to the Bhootanese, who in the old days of a strong ruler in Assam appear to have been kept in good order, probably by drastic measures, are the Akas—a small tribe allied to the Nagas on the south side of the Brahmaputra,—and who had a reputation for violence. When the English first came into contact with them was in 1829, when the depredations of the Tāgi Raja necessitated action being taken against him. He was captured and got four years in the Gauhati jail, which it was thought would teach him better ways. But on release he at once turned to the old game, eluding re-capture; and in 1835 he and a strong following treacherously obtained entrance to the Baliapara stockade, held by a small garrison of Assam Light Infantry (now the 6th Goorkha Rifles), and managed to cut up twenty-four people. Instead of a punitive expedition a blockade of the tribe was started, lasting some seven years, during which time the Tāgi Raja and his following maintained a guerrilla warfare, evading capture until he vanished quietly from the scene. In 1875 trouble again broke out over boundary demarcations, and a small expedition was sent into the hills, but with no success. On this followed another blockade, which brought the tribe to its senses a few years later. In 1883, when the Calcutta Exhibition was coming off, a native official was sent to the Aka chief to ask him to supply articles for the exhibition, and also for a man and a woman to be sent down to be modelled there. The chief took offence at the request and detained the official. This act was immediately followed by a serious raid on Baliapara, when two forest officials were captured amongst many others; and a British force consisting of 700 rifles of the 43rd Assam Light Infantry and 12th B.I., with two guns of the Kohat mountain battery and 450 transport coolies under command of General Sale Hill, entered the Aka country in December, 1883. The advance was rapid and was opposed at the Bharali river, where the tribesmen attacked the camp at night, causing us one killed and seven wounded. A few days later the principal village Mehdi, strongly stockaded, was attacked and assaulted. The guns taking the heart out of the Akas, they did not wait for the bayonet, but broke and fled. Two days later they sent in their captives, and in January, 1884, the force was withdrawn on the Akas entering into an agreement with Government to report their arrival at any markets in the plains, where they would fairly barter their goods, and not thieve or commit crimes in our territory, or join any parties who may hereafter become enemies of the British, to appear in the plains without weapons, to recover debts from our ryots through our civil court, and to forfeit the pensions to their chiefs should these terms not be abided by.

DAPHLAS AND MIRRIS.

The next tribes immediately to the east of the Akas are the Daphlas and Mirris, the latter of whom have never given us trouble and stand in some sort of servile relation to their powerful neighbours the Abors; while the former tribe, with whom we first came in contact in 1835 has given in earlier days a good deal of annoyance. Their country which, like the rest of the border is hilly and densely forest clad, is much more accessible than that of the neighbouring tribes; while one tribal sub-division, the Apa Tanangs, own a magnificent elevated plateau laid out in highly cultivated terraces, which was once visited by the late Mr. Macabe, who also found their country full of articles of Chinese manufacture; though what communication there may be between the Daphlas and Thibet or China we do not know. The Daphlas and Apa Tanangs are thought to number some 25,000, and when we arrived in Assam they had a formidable reputation which, however, did not survive a close acquaintance. This reputation had come down from early days when the Ahoms from 1646 on, had to send several expeditions into their hills, when it not unfrequently happened the Daphlas were successful until a very large force crushed out all opposition. In 1673 Ahom "buranjis" record an Ahom force being sent to exact reparation for raids made into the plains, and which came utterly to grief, being surrounded by the Daphlas and almost annihilated.

In 1758 the Ahoms, in order to check their raiding propensities, found it necessary actually to erect forts along the foot of the hills and institute a long blockade of the tribe; which goes to show that the tribe possessed brave and warlike propensities in the past, though these exist no longer. Mahomed Kasim, a Moghul historian of the seventh century, speaks of this tribe as being "entirely independent of the Ahom king, and whenever they find an opportunity plunder all the lands in the vicinity of their mountains."

It seems that the Daphlas, under the Ahom rule, had the right to levy what was called "Posa" directly from the ryots, in some cases this being paid in cash, in others in kind. This "Posa" has been sometimes alluded to as blackmail, which is inaccurate, it being rather of the nature of a well-ascertained revenue payment on account of which a corresponding remission was made in the State demand upon the persons satisfying it; it was a distinct feature in the Ahom revenue system, was not exacted from every tribe, and was at first not interfered with by the British officials, who avoided making any very radical changes. In time efforts were made to induce the tribe to resign this right, which was not complied with, and for many years constituted a difficulty. In 1835 a serious raid constrained offensive action on our part, when Captain Mathie, in charge of the Darrang district, led a small military force into the hills where, after a little desultory fighting, certain captives were released, and a series of outposts established along the border. After this, certain sections of the Daphla tribe submitted and agreed to resign their right to collect "Posa," which for many years was entirely stopped; till it was found the Daphlas we were concerned with, being subordinate to a stronger community in the higher ranges, these latter were oppressing the former, who now had no money to pay them with as formerly had been customary. The Government then in 1862 directed the "Posa" to be changed to a monetary payment of Rs. 4,000 annually on their chiefs agreeing not to aid the enemies of the British Raj, to arrest offenders, and to arrange that one chief should live near the British official to be the medium of communication with the Daphlas. All went well until 1871, when the tribe again gave trouble, which started in a curious way. A severe epidemic of whooping-cough occurred amongst the Daphlas living on and in our border which spread to the hill villages. These latter demanded compensation from the men on the low hills and plains, amongst whom the malady started. As this was refused the hill Daphlas raided a village on the border, killing a number and carrying off thirty-five persons. A British force was at once ordered to assemble, but interminable delays took place owing to disagreements between the civil and military authorities; and eventually a column of 600 rifles of the 44th A.L.I. (now the 8th G.R.) were advanced to the border under Major Cory. The villages concerned were but five marches beyond our border, and the country is, as before stated, the most easily accessible of all the north-east tribes. Unfortunately, the sound forward designs of Cory were over-ridden by the less advanced policy of the civil authorities; and, as is so often the case in divided counsels, the result ensued that nothing was done beyond a long and futile blockade. In early 1874, therefore, Colonel Stafford with a column of 1,000 rifles, three mountain guns, and 1,500 coolies entered the hills. The Daphlas made no resistance, but paid up fines and returned the captives. Little or nothing was done by this large force in exploration or survey, and it returned to Assam

GROUP OF ĀBORS.

amidst a clamour from Government over wasted money. But it was projected on a ridiculously large scale by the civil authorities, by whom also it was controlled and accounted a political success, though subsequent events have shown that no such serious measures had really ever been needed. In 1896 the Apa Tanang section began raiding on a small scale, which was soon stopped by Captain Roe with a small force of the Dibrughar Military Police

Battalion making a promenade through their hills, and which was sufficient to make them pay up their fines at once. This has proved the last of the trouble with this tribe, any further offences having been simply of a nature to be settled by police.

The Ābors.

We now come to the two tribes round whom at present the chief interest centres, namely, the Ābors and Mishmis. The former occupies the mountainous region between the Dihang (Tsan Po) and the Dibong rivers, and next to the Naga tribes on the south side of the Brahmaputra valley, are the most formidable and physically superior to their neighbours. The Mirris, dwelling between the Daphlas and Ābors, are allied to the latter, and are so alike that it seems evident they both came from the same original home—wherever that was ; the Mirris, migrating first and having been longer influenced by association with the plains folk, have lost their savagery and hardihood, which the later arrivals, the Ābors, have retained. Intercourse between the two tribes is intimate, which does not seem to exist between the others, who live entirely independent of each other. That all own some sort of subordination to the more remote races living further into the Himalayas to the north of them seems certain, but who these are and where their different boundaries lie we have no definite knowledge ; nor is any knowledge forthcoming as to when they settled in these hills, which history shows had once a strong, thriving, and almost civilised race dwelling in large cities along the outer ranges of hills now inhabited by wild Ābors and Mishmis. The Ahom "buranjis" are silent as to any trouble having occurred with these two races. The Ābors are said not to fear the Thibetans, and trade much with them, their markets being more accessible than ours. Captain Neufville in 1825 first makes mention of the Mirris as living in the plains and low hills from the Sisi district of Lakhimpur almost to the Dihang river, where they

JANAKMUKH POST, DIHANG RIVER, AND DISTANT ĀBOR HILLS.

merge into the Ābors, while the Bor Ābors occupy the inner and loftier ranges of hills which from the plains up are covered with dense forest. As various expeditions have merely penetrated the outer fringe of hills, what lies beyond is utterly unknown to us, though much information was expected on this point from the recent expedition of 1911–12, and from exploration work going on the following winter. It is stated the Ābors can turn out some 10,000 to 15,000 fighting-men, and the feeble conduct of troops and officials in the past has encouraged them to think the most of their powers.

The Ābors are divided into four clans, Menyong, Panghi, Padam, and Shimong, the two former dwelling between the Yamne and Dihang rivers and west of the latter river; the Padam east of the Yamne; and the Shimong to the north up the left bank of the Dihang. The character of the country is most difficult—entirely mountainous and forest-clad, with the rivers running for miles through rocky gorges, and unnavigable above Pasighat. Communications are only by means of the roughest tracks from village to village, and the rainfall in this region is exceedingly heavy, the only open months for work being October to the end of March. Their weapons are a long, straight "dao," which comes from Thibet, spears, and bows and arrows, the latter being prepared for war with a dab of poisoned paste made sometimes of pig's blood and aconite or the juice of the croton plant, which is put on just behind the arrow head. In most cases, however, from being made up for some time the poison loses its deadly efficacy, though it still makes a festering wound. A few old Tower muskets and muzzle-loading guns are also found in most villages.

Unlike Singphos and Nagas, they do not stockade their villages, but build these defences at a distance to command all approaches, behind which they have frequently stood very stoutly. Like all these savage tribes they rely mostly on night attacks, ambuscades, booby traps, and stone shoots, etc., on which they will expend great labour. The religion of this tribe is purely animistic. It was in 1826 that the Ābors were first visited by Englishmen, Messrs. Bedford and Wilcox, in a friendly way, who went to Membu, which they reported on as being the most important

CLEARING FOREST FOR CAMP GROUND IN THE ĀBOR COUNTRY.

of the tribal settlements and numbering 300 odd houses. Some years after this an early Political Agent with a strong vein of optimism describes the Ābors as being the most powerful and best disposed of all the hill tribes—which description was not long after shown to be wholly incorrect as regards their disposition.

Trouble first occurred with the tribe in 1848 over what they considered their inalienable rights over the Mirris, as well as to all fish and gold found in the streams issuing from their hills. The Assam Government had already begun to acquire considerable revenue from the gold dust of these rivers, which industry had long been carried on by Hindu gold washers who gave conciliatory offerings of the dust to the Ābors. The Ābors, finding these offerings decreasing as the Hindu washers realised their new position, the tribe raided into the plains and carried off a number of these gold washers. This necessitated Major Vetch, on duty at Sadiya, taking a force across the border. At first there was no opposition and the captives were given up, on which Vetch began to retire, and had his camp seriously attacked that night. The Ābors were beaten off, but the troops re-crossed the border unwilling to risk anything further.

In the succeeding years a number of outrages occurred, culminating in 1858 in a serious attack on a village but six miles from Dibrughar. Kebang village headed this raid, and an expedition at once set out under Major Lowther, with 110 rifles and two howitzers, to punish this village, which lies some twenty to thirty miles above Pasighat on the border. With this force went the Deputy Commissioner, whose presence and authority tied Lowther's hands, and various disagreements occurred. The Deputy Commissioner placed too much reliance on information with which he furnished the commander of the column, and which was faulty. A point four miles from Kebang village was reached, where a stockade was met with from which fire was opened and a bugler killed. The approach being difficult, the force withdrew to renew the attack next day; but that night the Ābors sturdily attacked the camp, the troops got demoralised and retired out of the hills. In doing so they were hustled the whole of the way, and lost four killed and twenty-two wounded. As all the neighbouring villages had now joined Kebang, the discomfited expedition made ignominious haste for Dibrughar. For this failure both Commander and Deputy Commissioner were severely blamed by the authorities.

The repulse of this force naturally encouraged the tribe to greater aggression, and in the following year, 1859, another force under Major Hannay, with 300 rifles of the 42nd A.L.I., sixty gunners with two howitzers and two mortars, were sent across the border to go for Kebang. This force advanced as the previous one had done to Pasighat, and thence attacked two stockaded positions at Runkang and Manku, where the Ābors were driven out with a loss to us of one killed and forty-four wounded. The savages stuck well to their defences, and this together with the difficult nature of the country and the great number of coolies and elephants with the column, took the heart out of Hannay and his men. After a halt of a few days it was thought advisable to clear out of the hills; so without any attempt to reach Kebang, the real objective, they retreated to the plains with results to their efforts as unsatisfactory as Lowther's had been.

Another determined raid in 1862 on another village near Dibrughar, and on the south side of the river, obliged a recourse to punitive measures again, and Colonel Garston led a force of similar strength to Hannay's against Runkang village. However, they only got as far as Lallichapri when the civil official arranging a meeting and parley, a treaty was patched up with the tribe, who agreed to respect the border on consideration of a "quid pro quo." As the arrangement of "Posa" had never existed between the Ahoms and Ābors, Government agreed to a similar custom as existed between it and the Daphlas; and the Ābors became the recipients of "Posa," consisting of iron hoes, salt, rum, opium, and tobacco; later this was turned into a monetary stipend of Rs. 3,400 annually. Small wonder that the Ābors after all these futile efforts at punishment on our part and their recent substantial gain should have had an exaggerated notion of their own powers. Their outrages in various petty ways still continued, and still they received their "Posa"!

In 1881 they crossed into the Mishmi country and practically controlled one of the trade routes into the interior, which necessitated a strong outpost of 300 rifles being located at Nizamghat, which overawed them for a time.

This unsatisfactory state of affairs and our apathy towards the offenders continued up to 1893, when one of our Mirri villages was raided by Pashi and Menyong Ābors, and captives were carried off. The usual negociations for their restitution were made with the usual empty results; so, as the behaviour of the Ābors, their insolence and disregard of Garston's treaty, was affecting the other tribes, notably the Mishmis, a fifth expedition was organised against them of 400 Military Police from Dibrughar, 100 rifles of the 44th Goorkha Rifles (now 8th G.R.) and 1,500 coolies for transport. This well-equipped force started across the border in January, 1894, under command of Captain Maxwell.

The Political Officer with the column directed the political side of the expedition and also controlled in a large measure its general management, which, as was only to be expected, produced disagreement and some friction. Bomjur, Dambuk, and Silluk were the first objectives, and the first village was taken at dawn on January the 14th without opposition. Dambuk was found strongly stockaded as usual a mile or so in front of the actual village. The dense forest prevented the possibility of any turning movement, and as the first efforts of the advance guard to rush the stockade failed, and the seven-pounder guns made no effect, a general assault was ordered. The Ābors fought well, standing to their defences, keeping up showers of arrows and stones while the attackers were hacking at the *chevaux de frise* of "panjis" or bamboo stakes, which prevented their reaching the stockade. At last the Ābors gave way and the defences were carried; too late though in the evening to make any further advance on the village, which next morning was found deserted. A move was now

A MORE CIVILISED FORM OF SUSPENSION BRIDGE MADE BY THE TROOPS IN THE ĀBOR COUNTRY.

made against the villages of Mimasipu and Silluk, both were destroyed, opposition only being met with at the latter place. The Political Officer now learnt that Damroh, a large village stated to be four long marches further into the hills, had also taken their share in the fighting, so an advance against it was decided on. Transport and supply difficulties now arose, and a halt was called until twenty days' rations could be collected at Bordak, to which place the force had advanced just below the junction of the Yamne and Dihang valleys. This was now made the base, while sick were returned to Bomjur, the starting-point of the expedition. The Political Officer, relying on local information, said it was quite unnecessary to leave a strong guard at Bordak, to which Maxwell disagreed, but as the management was in the hands of the former, he gave in to the extent of a small guard composed of weakly men under a native officer, himself not fit. After nearly a month's delay the rations were collected and the force advanced, leaving seventeen rifles and forty-four coolies at Bordak; rations were to be sent on by Ābor coolies. Dukku, two marches on, was reached without mishap, and next day only six miles were made owing to the difficult nature of the country, and a reconnoitring party up the Yamne gorge was fired upon. The next march only two miles were covered, and further difficulties were experienced owing to the Ābor coolies deserting. The column was now in straits; they had been far longer on the road than had been anticipated, and no supplies had reached them from the base. An attempt was made to reach Damroh with a flying column, now only some four miles off, and which was to destroy the place and return the same day. This, however, failed, the march being greatly delayed by having to turn the enemy out of a great stone "shoot" arranged far up on the hill side. So this column returned at two o'clock in the day without having reached its objective. The whole force had now to turn back, no rations having come out from Bordak, and *en route* the Ābors opposed the retreat at Silli and Dukku.

Bordak was duly reached, only to be found completely gutted, dead bodies strewing the camp and the stores mostly destroyed. It transpired from the one man alone who escaped the massacre that the enemy had come into the camp in the guise of carriers who were expected, and that while loads were being distributed to them they suddenly set upon the small guard, cutting down all right and left. This now decided the Political Officer to leave the country, but Maxwell persuaded him to stay long enough to punish Padu and Membu villages, which must have been concerned in the destruction of the Bordak camp. Both villages were burnt with but little opposition, and the force withdrew to Sadiya by the end of March.

The objects of this expedition can only be said to have been half accomplished and at a very considerable loss to us, namely, forty-nine killed and forty-five wounded. Of course the "Posa" or annual monetary stipend has been stopped since this, and with one exception, that of an insignificant raid in 1903, this tribe has given no further trouble until March, 1911.

CHAPTER X

Mr. Noel Williamson, who had been Political Officer at Sadiya since 1904, had got on terms of friendliness with both the Ābors and Mishmis, and had made one or two trips into the country of the latter with intent to reach Rima, but had not succeeded. He was a man of extraordinary tact and geniality, and from having been long in the Lushai and Naga countries, and also at Sadiya, he had acquired considerable insight into the characteristics of these various savage peoples. Their friendship he had gained while yet maintaining a strong hand, and he was looked upon as one of the best of our border officers. In 1909 he and Mr. Lumsden had made a trip into the Ābor hills to Kebang, and had been invited to pay another visit. This was done a year later when Williamson and Dr. Gregorson went into the hills, hoping in the friendly attitude of the tribesmen to be able to push up the Dihang river into the unknown hinterland and discover the supposed falls in that river which a former native explorer, Kinthup, reported in 1882 as existing. This Kinthup travelled down the Tsan Po from Thibet, and was taken captive twice for periods of several months, but eventually reached a point north of the Ābor country which he surmised must have been only thirty-five miles from the plains of Assam. He saw the falls near a place called Gyala Sindong, but was constrained to return to Thibet. In March, 1911, both Williamson and Gregorson and their party came to grief, being treacherously cut down by Kebang Ābors of the Menyong clan just after their arrival at a village, Komsing, only two or three managing to escape.

To punish the Ābors and also to explore and survey this country, for, owing to China's movements in Thibet and along the south-eastern borders of that country, a real interest was at last being awakened in this long stretch of unknown borderland, a large force under the command of Major-General Bowers, C.B., consisting of the 1st Battn. 2nd Goorkhas, 1st Battn. 8th Goorkha Rifles, 32nd Sikh Pioneers, a company of Sappers and Miners, a Signal Company and the Lakhimpur Military Police Battalion, with usual staff and two seven-pounder guns and the Maxim detachment of the Assam Valley Light Horse, concentrated at Kobo, forty-five miles above Dibrughar on the Brahmaputra, where the base was established in October, 1911. With this force also went 3,000 Naga transport carriers. During the summer the Military Police Battalion had made a forward move at once on hearing of the massacre, had rescued the survivors, and made a capital reconnaissance viâ Ledum and Mishing, when they were recalled by Government; otherwise it is probable they would have been able to effect seasonable and immediate punishment of Kebang. They were, however, allowed to build and hold a strong stockaded post at Balek throughout the rains, thus holding the tribe in check. The rainy season was exceptionally severe and long, and it was not till near the end of October that the forward move could be made in two columns, the main one moving up the Dihang valley to Pasighat and Kebang, while a smaller column of 500 rifles marched to Ledum and Mishing to protect the left of the main column, as the attitude of the neighbouring tribe of Galongs, who are more allied to the Mirris than to the Ābors, was uncertain.

The official objects of this expedition were to punish the Kebang and Komsing villages concerned in the massacre, to reduce all clans to submission throughout the country so as to facilitate survey and exploration work, and to visit all the principal villages. The Dihang was to be explored as far as the falls, and information obtained enabling a suitable boundary to be adopted with Thibet and China. The Ledum column having no tracks to follow, which was not the case with the main column, had to practically cut every mile of their advance through the densest jungle, and while the reconnoitring party was pushing up to Mishing the first contact with the Ābors was made, the 2nd Goorkha scouts surprising and killing a picquet. Mishing was later occupied, and till the end of November nothing but small reconnaissances were feasible owing to stringent orders from head-quarters which forbade any night to be spent out of camp. This for a long time obviated any chance of active offence or wide reconnaissance work, and lost more than one chance of bringing the enemy to book ; and the column had to content itself with rapid marches out and back in all directions, in which on two or three occasions they were able to surprise

NATIVE CANE BRIDGE OF THE ĀBOR AND MISHMI COUNTRIES.

the enemy's ambuscading parties. At the end of November these orders as to sleeping in the Mishing Post were relaxed, and two small columns were despatched against Korang village in the Galong country. In November a strong reconnoitring party from Mishing, along the Dihang and Kebang path, not being allowed to combine with the main force, the opportunity of well punishing the Ābors at Kekyar Monying, where nearly a fortnight was spent, was lost. Parties were also now able to scour the country almost as far as Rotang, where it was anticipated a junction would be made with the main column.

This latter force had in the meantime concentrated at Pasighat on the 26th of October, and stockades were built here and at Janakmukh on the line of communication. On the 6th of November the force reached the Sirpo river with no opposition, due probably to the activity of the Ledum column, ahead of, and on the left flank of, the main column. On the 7th of November a reconnaissance came into contact with the enemy, who were punished severely with a casualty list to us of an officer severely wounded in the thigh by a poisoned arrow, two riflemen killed, and one wounded. Road-making by the pioneers and sappers was going on slowly, contending, as these had to, with ceaseless difficulties of gorge, jungle, and hill side; and the troops were more or less held back until the efforts of the road-makers permitted a short advance. On the 19th of November Rotang village was reached, in front of which a large stockade on the Igar stream was found and attacked by the 8th G.R. in front and flank, who were received by a fall of stones from "shoots" above, and a fire of guns and arrows. A flanking party, after a severe climb, succeeded in capturing the stockade with a few casualties in several wounded by the stone "shoots" and one by a gunshot. Ten days were spent at Rotang roadmaking, collecting supplies and reconnoitring. As the main column was now abreast of the Ledum one, this was broken up, and after locating two companies of Military Police to hold Mishing, it was ordered to march across the hills and join headquarters at Rotang, which was done after three days' severe marching in heavy rain. The large stockade at Kekyar Monying was now found barring a continuation of the advance up the Dihang, and a force of one company 2nd Gs. and three companies 8th G.R. with the Maxim detachment of the Assam Valley Light Horse were sent across the Dihang on the 3rd of December, the sappers managing with great labour to get a hawser over to the other bank, and by 11 p.m. the little force was across. It was, however, charged by Ābors in the dark as it crawled through the forest, when two riflemen of the 2nd Gs. were cut down and killed by a party of Ābors who got close in. Next morning, this force having got into position and the left flank attack being also nearly ready, the whole advanced, and the great stockade was easily captured, thirty Ābors being killed, with no loss to us. Five days more were spent here, and on the 9th of December, Kebang, the main objective for punishment, was reached, sixty-two miles from the border which the force had left on the 22nd of October. It was found deserted, a condition about which there had never been much doubt; and after its destruction a wing of the 8th G.R. pushed on to Yemsing, cutting its way through the jungle instead of going by the main path, with the result that they surprised and inflicted loss on the enemy. The first phase of the expedition was now over, but although Kebang had been reached and destroyed it was found the Menyong Ābors had only vanished into their forests and showed no signs of submission, as was evidenced by many cases of convoys being fired on and telegraph wire cut. More activity being now displayed in scouring the country round Yemsing and Kebang, large amounts of grain and cattle were captured and a few small hostile parties dispersed; while, in the early days of 1912, the Ābors came in seeking peace when they realised most of their villages were occupied and food supplies carried off, in addition to losing possibly 200 men. Punitive operations now being considered at an end, those who had chiefly participated in Mr. Noel Williamson's massacre having been given up, tried and sentenced, and looted rifles returned, attention was directed to survey and exploration.

When the force crossed the border it was not known what the attitude of the various other clans would be. Rumour said the Panghi and Padam clans would join with the Menyongs, but these, having had no hand in the massacre, though hostile, were not so openly; merely sitting on the fence for a time, as it were, until they realised the desirability of professing unswerving friendship to us.

At the end of December then, two exploration and survey columns left headquarters, one to move through the Panghi and Padam Ābor country under Colonel Macintyre with 100 rifles 2nd Goorkhas and carriers for supplies, and which, after visiting all the principal villages as far as Damroh a large one of 800 houses, completed a very successful tour by early March.

The other one, under a civil official, with 100 rifles 8th G.R. and carriers for twenty-four days' supplies, went up the Dihang to survey the course of that river, but can hardly be said to have met with conspicuous success. On one occasion, at Shimong, it was touch and go whether another regrettable incident, even possibly a massacre, might not have taken place, which was fortunately averted by the timely arrival of a party of troops, this occasion having arisen through our mistaken and over-friendly attitude to a people of doubtful intentions. Rain and mist interfered with survey work, and the Naga coolies were greatly exhausted with marching. However, this party did make a dash and got some distance beyond Shimong, which was found to be, with its sister village of Karko, a sort of barrier between Thibet and Assam; these two strong villages on either side of the Dihang, allowing no Thibetans to pass south and no Ābors or Assamese to pass up. From here a broadish, well-defined trade path led towards Thibet, trodden by hundreds of laden yāk bringing commodities to Shimong, whose inhabitants distributed the same throughout the northern Ābor clans. Another yāk road was also noticed leading up the Siyom river below Karko. A certain amount of work was done by this party, who fairly well established the identity of the Tsan Po with the Dihang, and consequently with the Brahmaputra. In late March, 1912, the Ābor force, originally consisting of eighty British officers and 3,000 fighting-men broke up and returned to India. The casualty lists showed twenty-one British officers sent to hospital sick, of whom one died, while 850 of other ranks were treated for sickness or wounds. Shortly after their return a medal was granted to this force. The veil of interest and mystery surrounding the course of the Tsan Po and its falls it was hoped would have been cleared up with exploration and surveys, and reports were eagerly looked forward to not only by us, but by geographers of all nations. Hopes, however, in these matters, entertained more heartily by none than by the Survey of India, were fated to be deferred; and this particular locality still remains about the least known of any in India or, indeed, in Asia.

Thus ended the sixth expedition against the Ābors, and we may now glance briefly at what each accomplished, or rather what most of them did not. We have seen how, between 1848 and 1893, five expeditions crossed the border. The first two failed utterly owing to the irresolution of their leaders; the third was ineffectual owing to divided counsels producing some friction between the two authorities with the force; the fourth only effected a treaty never respected by the tribesmen; while the fifth also suffered in its arrangements and energy due as before to divided counsels which, when permitted to exist, can never make for a harmonious and successful issue to expeditionary work. With the sixth, the expedition we have just dealt with, Government has expressed its satisfaction, and as nothing was said about the expense stated by Sir F. Wilson to have been £124,300 (including the small Mishmi mission), we can presume it was thought rightly spent. But it has been found still necessary to complete the work expected of it by large survey parties and strong escorts entering those hills again in the winter of 1912–13. These, however, through various delays in the making of preliminary arrangements always in these wild border countries no very

MISHING STOCKADE—LEAF AND BAMBOO SHELTERS FOR OUR MEN—ABOR COUNTRY.

easy matter, were allowed to start only very late in an unexpectedly good and dry season, whereby they could not accomplish all that was desired, and the work will probably be seen continued through the winter, 1913–14. It is generally said that dual control exists no longer, and that commanders conduct their own operations and see to their own political business. In a sense it is true, but in another sense it is not, and commanders now find themselves controlled throughout by telegraph by those who have never been near the scene of operations or have any notion of the people to be dealt with. It can hardly be said in favour of this system that it engenders the confidence of a commander in himself or calls forth his best efforts. In spite of all labour expended on a good mule road and stockades built to be garrisoned by Military Police, which was the original intention, with a view to dominating the country instead of merely going in and coming out of the hills, final orders on breaking up of the force showed to the regret of all ranks that this intention had been abandoned. It had been hoped that the post at Rotang would have been instrumental in putting a stop to slave trading and other cruel practices of these savage tribes, and the final decision was the more disappointing because the Ābors (particularly the Panghi section) having learnt during our stay to appreciate some of the blessings of civilisation, were anxious for a trading post and the benefits of a hospital. Whether this policy is likely to produce good effects only the future can show. Past history here does not offer much hope of permanent friendly relations and good behaviour unless we recast our methods in dealing with these frontier tribes.

Of all hill expeditions of modern times, at least on the eastern side of India, General Penn Symond's action in putting down the disorders in the Chin hills in 1889–90, can well be held up as an example of successful operations of that nature, when he overran the country with small columns, giving neither himself, his troops, nor the enemy, any rest until all opposition ceased. Even with him an effort at dual control threatened to cause trouble, which did occur once only in the south of those hills. As to resolution and the lack of it, Lieutenant Eden's famous exploit (which is dealt with in the Mishmi account) in 1854 shows us what the former quality can effect; while a different tale would have been told of Manipur in March, 1891, had that quality prevailed and the Military head been supreme.

It will be said that the foregoing remarks on the expeditions show only a carping criticism, without offering suggestions for improved future methods. But with the example of history before us what more is needed? It is known that in 1899 Mr. Needham, the knowledgeable man on the spot, declared a force of some sixty rifles to be ample for the purpose of entering these hills to exact punishment from a weak tribe; his advice went unheeded, with the result of money wasted and nothing done, the force sent in being too big and unwieldy. In this connection it is an open secret that this particular expedition fell under Lord Curzon's scathing condemnation, in which he is said to have pointed out that had the original suggested smaller force gone up, all results would have been achieved at a cost of a few thousand rupees instead of lakhs. This would point to an absence of accurate knowledge as to the capability of the tribe to be dealt with on the part of the controlling powers. It would appear to have been better in 1911 if, in dealing with these little-known tribes and their countries, the advice of the few, who, from their official position, were most intimately acquainted with them and with what is requisite in the nature of expeditionary work, had prevailed. Of course it is always easy to criticise and to find fault; but it certainly does seem as if expeditions in the past, under faulty arrangements and this dual control, had failed; while present day ones, though showing greater improvements in method, may be said to err on the side of being unwieldy in size and over-elaborate in arrangements, while far distant control of matters is still also considered necessary.

In the case of this last expedition, 1911–12, the tribes, in spite of their inflated idea of power, never attempted to put up any fight against a large, slow-moving force, knowing how futile their efforts would have been; which points to the correctness of the statements of those who knew and those who were with the force, namely, that one battalion of Military Police with a backing of, say, two companies of Goorkha regulars, could have rapidly done all punitive work early, while roadmaking went on behind. As soon then as opposition was over, probably in a fortnight to three weeks, these Military Police and Goorkhas would then have sufficed for escorts to the survey parties which might then have ranged the country.

These considerations surely point to the necessity of the authorities with whom the final responsibility as to what action in each case is to be taken must rest, being supplied with the best and most reliable information, not only from the Civil authority, but also from thoroughly qualified Military officers well acquainted with all local conditions. Can it be said that the recent withdrawal of the General Officer Commanding and staff from the former Assam

Brigade and the transfer of their duties to the already overburdened General Officer Commanding at Lucknow, a week's hard travelling from any scenes of these border operations, has tended towards efficiency in this respect ?

In contrary distinction to this somewhat retrograde action on the part of the Military, the Civil authorities, fully recognising the growing importance of this borderland, have recently formed a Political Agency with headquarters at Sadiya. The Assistant Political Officer there, formerly subordinate to the Deputy-Commissioner at Dibrughar, having been replaced by a Political Officer working directly under the orders of the Chief Commissioner of Assam. This officer has now under him three English assistants, each of whom is in charge of a particular tribe, and the duties of these officers are to extend British influence without stirring up hostility by needless interference with tribal customs. The particular officer chosen for this new duty shows that the so often misinterpreted term " selection " has been most satisfactorily applied in this case ; Mr. Dundas having done sixteen uniformly successful years among tribes on this border. It is therefore not unreasonable to suppose that this new action will be productive of the best results.

As before stated, the work of exploring and surveying the Dihang valley and northern Ābor country having been but slightly touched upon in the winter of 1911–12, this has again been carried on by strong parties of Military Police and Royal Engineers throughout that of 1912–13 ; the work having been started again in the neighbourhood of Kebang above which one party worked west and north up the Siyom river, while another continued far up the Dihang, hoping to reach Pemakoi peak and possible even the great falls of the Tsan Po. Both parties were expected to

TYPICAL ĀBORS WITH WOODEN HELMETS.

meet eventually near Pankang and Janbo before the close of the working season, when a considerable amount of ground would have been covered and mapped, and probably some definite idea of a frontier decided upon. Recent reports on the work of the various parties out surveying and exploring in these difficult mountainous regions show that much has been done to open up the country. From early December, 1912, the Ābor surveys carried out most valuable work under the able political direction and management of Mr. Dundas, extending their operations until late in the rainy season, 1913, and not returning to civilisation till mid August, 1913, after enduring discomfort and hardships which can only be realised by those who have lived in that corner of India. By them accurate survey was carried out as far north as latitude 29° 30′, and as far west as longitude 94° 30′, while the officers were able to cross the main Himalayan range by the Doshung-la, and to carry plane tabling beyond the above northerly limit, whereby they were able to establish the identity of the Tsan Po with the Dihang river beyond all doubt.

It was found that the Tsan Po breaks through the main range a little north-east of a lofty mountain, "Namchia Barwa," about latitude 29° 7′ and longitude 95° 3′, and 25,741 feet high, by a stupendous gorge which has probably never been traversed by any human being. No possible track exists through the gorge on either bank. The river, after passing through this, bends towards the south. The statement of the explorer Kinthup, who came far down the Tsan Po in 1882, till close to the Ābor hills regarding the existence of falls on this great river has not yet been verified; but his evidence has been corroborated in so many particulars by the Ābor surveys that there seems little reason to doubt his veracity as to their existing. The operations have now completed our geographical knowledge of these frontier regions east of longitude 95°, and with the return of Captain Bailey, whose intention is to reach Assam through eastern Bhutan, the gap left between longitude 95° and Bhutan will be filled in.

That he and his companion, Captain Morshead, have carried out their intention we now know, for in November, 1913, they emerged once more into Assam near Dewangiri, having been as far up the Tsan Po as they possibly could, and no doubt put up with very great hardships in penetrating one of the last of the few "secret places of the earth." Their reports, when published, should be full of interest. At present all that has been made public of their Tsan Po experiences is that they found no falls at all, only a series of long stretches of rapids. It seems not unlikely that they were not able to get as far up as the locality where the native explorer Kinthup saw them in 1882, where a certain Chinese Captain stated he saw them on his way to Pomed, or where a Thibetan Lama gave evidence to Colonel Waddell of them, in proximity to a large and ancient monastery situated just below these falls. The latter officer had met many Thibetans when in that country who had seen the falls and even recognised a rough sketch of them drawn by his friend the Lama. They also stated the locality to be one for pilgrimages to be made to, in order to propitiate a "King Devil" resident in the rush of the waters. So that it is yet possible the mystery surrounding this particular locality remains still to be solved.

It was found during the winter 1912–13 that the Abors now thoroughly realising that we can and mean to go into their hills, and having received certain lessons in the previous winter, had taken these to heart; for no serious molestation to parties was offered, or hindrance to work. Of course they have often tried the old game of "bluff," which, however, invariably subsided at the last moment.

An experience of one of these parties may be mentioned as showing what patience, tact, and firmness is required in dealing with these folk. A party under Captain P. consisted of forty-six Military Police Sepoys and Surveyors, and when far into the

CONVOY CROSSING A STREAM IN THE ĀBOR COUNTRY.

hills reached a point where the Ābors seemed disposed to dispute any further advance. The tribesmen, to prevent us crossing the river, had cut away the long swinging cane bridge just before our party arrived; and when these started to build rafts with which to cross over, the Ābors began firing at them with bows and arrows from the forest and from across the river. No damage was done, and our Sepoys took no notice of this hostility. At last, just before the rafts were ready, the Ābors sent an emissary who enquired why no notice was taken of their arrows, and when were we going to fight? The interpreter explained that fighting was not our intention, that we were quietly touring through the hills, and that early next morning we should cross the river to their village, whereupon the Ābors quietly withdrew. Next morning the crossing was effected and the Ābors came forward to make friends, confessing their foolishness in attempting hostility, or to stop us; for which they now found themselves punished in that all their "jhooms" (cultivation) lay on the far side of the river, the bridge across which they had cut away, while our people had used all the canes and cut all trees suitable for anchoring the strands of a fresh bridge in order to make their rafts. So the Ābors were confronted by the tedious and difficult task of making a fresh cane bridge to cross by higher up. This sort of "bluff" was often met with and treated calmly, as in this instance.

An immense amount of country has now been surveyed up to and beyond the main watershed of the Himalayas in their locality, and great interest centres round the party under Captain Bailey, who alone are now left in the country, and who are working their way up the Tsan Po river.

That there are large falls on this great river received confirmation in a curious way. As stated before, it was hoped the expedition of 1911–12 might have been able to penetrate up to the Pomed border and possibly to locate the falls. Had they done so, it is now known they probably would have met the Chinese, when boundary matters might have had a satisfactory start. For amongst the Chinese troops recently expelled from Thibet, who were allowed passage to their own land through India, was an officer of the Celestial forces who had been with them in Pomed, who while they were there heard of the movement of General Bowers' expedition and expected they might meet each other, and who also substantiated the existence of the Tsan Po falls as he and his troops camped in their vicinity.

Before leaving the Ābors it would not be out of place to touch on questions that were asked in Parliament querying Mr. Williamson's presence in their hills, and expressions of disapproval made as to the need of sending a punitive expedition at all, seeing he was murdered in a locality where, the questioners state, he had no right to be. People arguing on those lines have no idea of the gross slur it would have been on us to have allowed such a massacre to pass unnoticed, simply from the outlook of economy and expense—which is really what their objections mean; nor do they realise what is required of a frontier official and his life. He has to be in touch with all tribes in his sphere of jurisdiction, to acquaint himself with all that is going on on either side of the border, and to influence, if possible, the wild folk in a right direction. For obvious reasons Government lays down rules as to the crossing of borders, and in 1872–73 a regulation was drawn up prescribing a limit of direct administration which is known as the "Inner Line," namely, a boundary maintained at the discretion of the Lieutenant-Governor, which British subjects of certain classes are not allowed to cross without a pass. This "Inner Line" shown on maps is not the British frontier—it is merely a line fixed by Government to guide the civil officers as to the extent of their jurisdiction. No frontier officer could adequately fulfil his duties if he sat year in year out in his headquarter station, so to speak, merely listening to most likely unreliable reports brought in by so-called "friendlies"! Would McCabe, Davis, Needham in Assam, and others in Burma have won such credit as border officials if they had not, when opportunity offered, accepted the responsibility for exceeding their routine instructions in order to get more in touch with wild people, whose customs and countries stimulated their keenest interest, and thereby gave Government a considerable amount of information obtainable in no other way?

CHAPTER XI

THE MISHMIS

THE Mishmis are the close neighbours of the Ābors, but are in no way kin to them, language and customs being entirely different. The Dibong river their western boundary, this tribe stretches north and east of Hkāmti Lông, where Mr. Ney Elias, a great authority on Burma border tribes, finds the Mishmis closely allied to the Khunongs, showing that the tribe now dealt with covers a very large area, though how far north they reach is not known ; but their country is generally said to be bounded on the north and east by the Thibetan provinces of Pomed and Zayul the fertile Lama valley, the capital of which is Rima.

The Mishmis who merge into the interest surrounding their Ābor neighbours do so by reason of a friendly mission sent into their country simultaneously with General Bowers' military expedition ; this was done in order to prevent the possibility of any of them joining in with the Ābors, for survey work, and also because of Chinese activity to the north and east of their hills, and amongst whom that nation had, it was reported, sent emissaries to claim their submission. This tribe is divided into four sections and are, on the whole, a weak race, the Meju and Chulikatta sections being, if the term can be applied, perhaps the most warlike. Like that of the Ābors, their country is extremely mountainous, covered with dense forests and vegetation, particularly in the outer and lower ranges, and is very difficult of access. Their original habitat is supposed to have been the highlands of north-east Thibet, whence, with the Chins, they moved south, remaining in their present locality while the other people moved further and spread out. Their general strength is unknown, but they are keen traders, greatly appreciating access to the markets in the plains, and are like almost all these tribes, worshippers of demons and evil spirits. The majority of the Mishmis acknowledge their dependence on us, though the Mejus consider themselves allies of Thibet, which feeling dates back to 1836, when the latter certainly assisted them against the Digarus.

This *terra incognita* has stimulated several explorers to penetrate their hills without much success, the first to do so being Lieutenant Burlton in 1825, who went up the Brahmaputra some distance above the Dihing river, and reported that "the people were very averse to receiving strangers." Two years later Lieutenant Wilcox succeeded in entering the Meju country, but the hostile attitude of one of the chiefs obliged him to return. In 1836 Dr. Griffiths went a little distance in, but was absolutely prevented from going further by the Mejus and certain Singphos, the latter, he states, seeming to have considerable influence over the Mishmis. He was followed in

A Mishmi Village and Warrior.

1845 by Lieutenant Rowlatt, who got as far in as the Du river, where he met Thibetans who turned him back at Tuppang village. In 1851 a French missionary M. Krick, made his way through the hills under the guidance of a Hkāmti chief, and, avoiding the land of the hostile chief, Jingsha, reached Walong. Here he was well received and had a good view of the Lama valley, but was not allowed to enter it. Three years later with a colleague M. Bourri, he again essayed to pass through the hills, and actually camped in the vicinity of Rima, when they were followed by another hostile chief, Kaisha, who, for motives of plunder, murdered both Frenchmen. On news of this outrage reaching India Lord Dalhousie, feeling something should be done in retribution, permitted Lieutenant Eden to undertake the work. Eden with a small party of twenty rifles of the Assam Light Infantry and forty Hkāmti volunteers with a few carriers, moved into the hills from Sadiya in February, 1855, and made one of, if not the most, successful of minor expeditions in all our punitive outings in Assam; for, after eight days' forced marching, swinging over dangerous torrents on bridges of single canes, experiencing bitter cold, and showing wonderful endurance of great hardships inseparable from rapidity of movement, in the grey dawn of a misty morning he reached and surprised Kaisha's village on the Du river with the aid of a friendly chief Lumling, who joined in just in time. After a sharp struggle, in which two of Kaisha's sons and many followers were killed in open fight, his people were dispersed. The greater part of the stolen property was recovered, as well as M. Krick's Singpho servant; and the victorious little party returned to Sadiya with the chief Kaisha, who was duly hanged in Dibrughar, but not before he had managed to kill two warders. Such an exploit did not fail to astonish and overawe the surrounding tribes. The completeness of Eden's success was, however, somewhat marred by Government's refusal to assist the chief Lumling, who shortly afterwards was set upon by a relative of Kaisha's who, with the aid of the Chulikatta section, completely exterminated the chief's family and people. Lumling was a Meju, and this action of the Government has led to a lasting and bitter feeling by that tribal section towards the British. Twelve years later, Mr. T. T. Cooper, when in their hills, found this feeling existing. Cooper was a political official in China, was deputed in 1870 to open a tea trade route from India to China, and found his way into south-west China, hoping to reach Assam viâ Bhatang and Rima. He, however, only got as far as the former place when he was arrested by Thibetan Lamas, and had to return after great hardhips, to Shanghai. In the following year he came to India to make the attempt from the Assam side, and at a meeting of the Chamber of Commerce in Calcutta several routes were discussed, chiefly those from Bhamo to Talifu; and from Bhamo through the Hukong valley to Dibrughar, and so to Calcutta. On this latter, proposals already had gone up for the Hukong valley to be properly surveyed. Cooper, however, favoured and explained the Mishmi route, which view the Chamber accepted, giving him Rs. 6,000 towards expenses of the journey. Any route lying through Thibet was known to be impracticable, as the Lamas monopolised the tea trade and had their own settled routes further west through Sikkim and Bhootan, and from the east (China) through Ta-chien-loo, and forbade private enterprise. Cooper journeyed up the Brahmaputra, reached the sacred shrine at Brahmakund, and with the help of a young Hkāmti chief, got as far as the Larkong mountain, which forms a defined boundary between Assam and Thibetan ground. He got no further, however, being stopped by two Thibetan officials and constrained to give up the attempt and return.

Cooper makes some interesting remarks on our border methods, and compares them with those adopted by the Chinese, condemns the blockade system to punish tribes as being calculated to produce lasting feelings of antagonism, and speaks of the wisdom of relieving the whole of northern Assam from invasion and violence by Government's system of " Posa " (which has been described before), which yearly expenditure of a few hundred pounds has produced useful and good effects. He favourably compares China's methods of dealing with her border tribes, with ours, stating that country centuries back began subjugating and making friends with them, distributing " Posa," and thus creating a capital system of frontier guards, as it were, along her distant boundaries. The chief of every tribe has also a nominal rank conferred upon him, and an annual stipend, while he is given an official dress which he is obliged to wear in the presence of Chinese functionaries.

In 1885, Mr. Needham, Political Agent at Sadiya,

reported that he had got through the hills and reached the district of Zayul. He was, however, not allowed near Rima when he got into its neighbourhood on his return.

The Mishmis have only once given a little trouble since 1855, namely, when the Bebejiya section murdered four people near Sadiya and carried off three persons and three guns. For this it was thought necessary to send a large force into the hills, and 1,200 troops with two mountain guns moved out from Sadiya on the 1st of December, 1899, returning on the 8th of February, 1900, having encountered no opposition (which, indeed, was never expected from the Bebejiyas). A small party only reached Hunli in the central valley which was deserted, and beyond a small amount of survey work and a large expenditure of money, namely, two and a half lakhs, it may well be said nothing was accomplished. On this occasion, it might be suggested, Lieutenant Eden's exploit could have been copied and would have sufficed.

In 1895 Prince H. d'Orléans made his adventurous journey from Tonkin across south-west China, eventually reaching Assam viâ Rima and Sadiya. No other European has been allowed through that town or country until Captain Bailey, late trade agent at Gyantze in Thibet, when in China in 1911 successfully managed his return to India by a long hazardous march viâ Bhatang to Rima and Sadiya. From his pen we may obtain some very interesting information as well as from the results of the exploring and road-making parties at work in this country throughout the winter of 1912–13. These latter were employed making a mule road up the Lohit valley to Walong, a place on the, at present, undefined frontier a little south-west of Rima, as well as exploring the valleys of the Dibang and Dri rivers further north in the Mishmi hills. And we now know from their reports, on completion of operations in these hills in late May, 1913, that the basin of the Dibang river has been completely surveyed and found to be shut in by a lofty mountain range which none of the rivers of Thibet break through. The making of bridle paths up the Lohit and Dibang valleys proved most laborious work, but was successfully carried out for many marches in each case.

The Hkāmtis

With these people and their neighbours, the Singphos, we reach the connecting link between the Assam and Burma border peoples. They are of the same race as the Ahoms with this difference, that they are Buddhists, and only arrived in the Sadiya district in the end of the eighteenth century, where, first settling on the Tengapani river, they crossed the Brahmaputra, ousted the Assamese governor of Sadiya and took that corner of Assam, where the British in 1825 left them alone on consideration of their agreeing to keep up a small force for the preservation of order. In 1825 they assisted us against the Singphos, and in 1835, on the death of the old Hkāmti chief, his son, openly disobeying our orders, was deported, and a British Political Agent was sent to Sadiya to administer the country.

Four years later, as we have previously seen, the

Hkāmtis rose and attacked Sadiya, killing Colonel White and many others. Since this they have never given further trouble. Their country, Bor Hkāmti, as the Assamese call it, and Hkāmti Lông by the Burmese, is very little known, though it has been visited a few times by Wilcox in 1828, by Woodthorpe and Macgregor in 1884, by Errol Gray in 1892, and in 1895 Prince H. d'Orléans passed through the northern corner of it; all of whom, with the exception of the latter, entered from the Assam side. Their country, somewhat less mountainous than those further west, possesses many broad, fertile, and well cultivated valleys; while they themselves are an intelligent and even literary folk, and far more civilised even than the Assamese. Prince H. d'Orléans remarks on their appearance, which strongly resembles that of the Laos towards French Indo-China, while the dress of their women is similar. Both sexes are great smokers, using a long pipe, often three feet long,

A SINGPHO OF THE EASTERN PATKOI.

with metal bowl, silver mouthpiece, and bamboo stem. The Hkāmtis are entirely an agricultural folk —rice, opium, and linseed being largely cultivated in the valleys. Their villages are always strongly stockaded, the houses inside rather crowded, and the numbers of temples and pagodas showing up among the surrounding forests, give a very picturesque note to the attractive and wild scenery. Some of their temples are of great size, one described by Mr. Errol Gray stands in a forest covered island in the Nam Kiu river, and is in regular Burmese style, ninety-five feet high and 125 feet in circumference at the base; four flights of stone steps lead up to the plinth on which it stands, each flight guarded by gigantic figures of fabulous beings. At each face of the compass on the plinth are four marble images of Buddha of excellent workmanship. Hkāmti Lông is connected with the outer world by two chief routes, the western one leading down the Nam Kiu to Assam, the south-eastern one 120 miles to Tamanthe on the Chindwyn river. The rainfall in these hills is very heavy and during the cold weather thick mists hang about, obstructing all views, often till mid-day.

Their neighbours, the Singphos, inhabit both sides of the Patkoi range, their old home having been in the Hukong valley on the south and east of that range. Here they are independent, and have been but rarely visited by Europeans. Roughly, their country is bounded by that of the Hkāmtis in the north, the Naga hills and Sadiya district on the west, the independent tribes of Upper Burma on the east, and Burma proper to the south. The Patkoi range rises to about 6,000 feet and is easy of passage, the passes being low and easy and the total distance across the range is only some seventy miles. The upper Chindwyn waters the Hukong valley, which is really a broad, fertile plain fifty miles in length by a varying breadth of fifteen to forty miles. Dense

TWO HEADMEN IN MĀSUNGJĀMI, WESTERN PATKOI.

forests cover the surrounding hills. The Singphos are identical with the Kachin (Chingpaw) of Burma, and are described as a fine athletic race, singularly honest, and not lacking in intelligence. They were addicted to raiding for slaves, of which they took a number from Assam, but it is averred never treated them badly. Every village looks after its own interests, only a few groups of villages are known to combine under one chief. It is believed they can turn out close on 10,000 fighting-men who are armed with spears, daos, and some matchlocks, for which a fair powder is made in the Hukong valley. At the time of the Burmese War this tribe had been worrying the Hkāmtis of Sadiya, who appealed to us for assistance. The Singphos, fearing they might be expelled from lands they valued in the Brahmaputra valley, came to treat with the British authorities. As this tribe deals largely in slaves, a procedure not tolerated by our Government, difficulties arose, and the Singphos suddenly joined in with the Burmese force advancing to reconquer Assam in May, 1825. These had reached the Noa Dihing and were met by Captain Neufville with 300 Sepoys and two gunboats, when in an action twenty-five miles from the mouth of the Dihing river he routed the Burmese with some loss, and followed them to Bisa on the west side of the Patkoi. At Dapha, a strong stockaded position held by some 300 Burmese and a few cavalry, was captured on the way; and near Bisa Neufville came on a large force of Burmese and Singphos drawn up in the open in line, with a force of cavalry on the right. At the time Neufville had but 200 Sepoys and some Hkāmti auxiliaries, but forming these into line, he attacked without hesitation. A few volleys created confusion amongst the cavalry, and a bayonet charge of his line ended the fight, the enemy broke and were pursued some miles. Neufville then held the Patkoi passes, while his Hkāmti and Moamaria allies scoured the country and put a stop to all Singpho opposition for a time. Ten years later the Dapha Gām, one of the four prominent Singpho chiefs, crossed the Patkoi

THE MORANG AT NOKCHING, WESTERN PATKOI, WITH HUGE CARVED SERPENT ON FRONT SUPPORTING TIMBER 35 FEET HIGH.

from the Hukong country and attacked the Gām of Bisa under our protection. To repel this invader, Captain Charlton was ordered out from Sadiya with 300 Sepoys, who had a stiff fight with the Dapha Gām's force on the way, and finally retook the Bisa stockades by assault, with losses on both sides. After this, for the better protection of this part of the country military posts were established at Bisa, Koogoo, and Ningroo. But for some years the Singphos were in a disturbed and discontented state due to their being deprived of their slaves; and in 1843 they broke out again. The Hukong men again came over, and both the Koogoo and Ningroo posts were sturdily attacked; but as there were British officers at these posts the enemy were beaten off. At Bisa, which was only held by a native officer's detachment, they succeeded in inflicting such loss that the native officer surrendered, upon which most of his men were killed at once and the remainder sold as slaves. A large force coming up from Assam the situation improved, and ended with severe punishment being inflicted on several turbulent villages, since when no further trouble has occurred in this part of the hills, and a few years later these posts were given up. The Singphos, however, not appreciating British rule, have largely returned to the Hukong country, where slavery still flourishes. In 1892 Mr. Needham visited this valley and found the people well disposed towards him; and in 1896, owing to the idea of linking Assam with upper Burma by railway, a survey party with a strong escort of the Lakhimpur Military Police Battalion from Dibrughar under Captain Roe crossed the Patkoi, went down the Hukong valley, and at Mayankwan joined hands with a similar survey party from Burma. No trouble was experienced here during this work. How far to the south of the Patkoi the Singphos extend is not known, but it is believed they largely form the inhabitants of the extensive tract of country lying between the upper Chindwyn and the Naga hills district, which is so-called "unadministered territory"—unmapped and unexplored. Two or three punitive expeditions

THE GREAT MORANG OR GUARD HOUSE IN MĀSUNGJĀMI VILLAGE, WESTERN PATKOI.

from the Naga hills have penetrated into this area a little way, and generally found opposition; and, in 1910, it was found necessary to send a small column from Kohima and one from Tamanthe, an outpost on the Chindwyn, against a strong village of Makwarri, a little north of the Saramethi peak. The two columns joined hands, punished Makwarri, and did a little survey work, but were not in the country long enough to effect much. The Burma Military Police found their way out of these hills by a more northern route, coming out on the Chindwyn at Heinsūn.

CHAPTER XII

BURMA BORDER TRIBES

WITH the last tribe we leave the portion of the north-eastern frontier administered by the Assam Government, and enter on the border lands controlled by that of Burma. In 1900, when the Upper Burma Gazetteer was published, the north and north-east boundaries had not been finally demarcated, and although since then several boundary commissions have been out, the entire line of frontier cannot be said to have been completely defined.

The results of surveying and exploration work done in 1911–12 and 1912–13 may complete the line, and will have revealed much of interest in the unknown country far beyond Myitkhyina towards Thibet, and also more to the north-east towards China. The length of this northern Burma border is roughly 540 miles from the Singpho hills on the west along the Chinese border of the Province of Yũnnan to the north-east, and the Chinese Shan States and French Indo-China to the east. Within these limits, and administered as semi-independent States, are the Northern Shan States, the Momeik (Möngmit) State and Hkāmti Lông State, which latter, with the Kachin hills north of the confluence of the Mali-Kha and Nmai-kha rivers, are only indirectly under our administration. In the Upper Chindwyn district are the two small States of Thaungthut and Sinkaling Hkāmti. Peculiar interest is given to these eastern borders by the fact that we are in this direction brought into direct touch with the Chinese, Siamese, and French. On the southern side of the Chinese boundary, the

SCENERY IN THE PATKOI RANGE NEAR HUKONG VALLEY, ABOUT 4,000 FEET EL.

Shan and Kachin hills are largely unadministered and unknown.

Upper Burma is arranged in natural divisions by its important rivers the Irrawadi, Chindwyn, and Salween, the first and last rising far beyond our confines in the unexplored tracts where India, Thibet, and China meet; while the Chindwyn rises nearer in, namely, in the hills south-west of Thama, whence as the Tanai, it flows through and drains the Hukong valley, and from whence on it is known as the Chindwyn. These rivers flow southward, and of those in the Kachin hills north of the confluence but little is known ; none of these seem navigable, and, except in the rains, all are fordable. This part of the province is encircled by walls of mountains densely forest-clad, and peopled by tribes of whom but little is known to us ; a few intrepid travellers, such as Cooper, Woodthorpe, Prince H. d'Orléans, and Errol Gray only having ventured far afield into them.

Of the two streams, the Mali-kha to the west and the Nmai-kha to the east, which unite some 150 miles above Myitkhyina to form the great Irrawadi, the former is navigable for country boats to a considerable distance, namely, up to Sawan, while the latter, owing to rapids is quite impracticable for any sort of boat. The course of the Nmai-kha is unknown at present. A little north of these regions the country was traversed by Prince H. d'Orléans and party in 1895 from Tonking to Sadiya. They were five months marching and struggling through this tangled mass of mountains, forests, and wild strange tribes, the country quite impracticable for baggage animals between the Salween and Irrawadi, until they got distant views of the snowy ranges beyond the Brahmaputra. Their delight at emerging from endless gloomy gorges into the more open Hkāmti Lông country leading down into the Assam valley can be well understood. The course of the Salween is stated to be unequalled for wild and magnificent scenery, which, flowing through stupendous gorges where it comes into British territory, is likened to that of a deep ditch with banks 3,000 to 6,000 feet high. The passes in these regions are all of considerable altitude, many being of 12,000 feet and over, while the Kachin hills, which merge northward into the high mountains just mentioned, present a mass of smaller ranges between the upper Chindwyn and upper Irrawadi running north and south and rising up to 6,000 feet or so, with no flat ground anywhere from the well-watered plain about Myithkyina, till the Hkāmti Lông country is reached, which is practically the upper valley of the

THE IRRAWADI AT MYITKHYINA.

Mali-kha. Beyond this, again, Mr. Errol Gray, who visited this locality in 1891, describes the view over this *terra incognita* as that of "a succession of ranges of forest-clad mountains spreading out like the fingers of the open hand to the south, converging to the north until massed in the high snows of the Thibetan ranges which stretch southwards and, covered with deep snow, limit the view to the east." This latter high range being the watershed between the Nmai-kha and Salween rivers. East of these Kachin hills and north to north-east of Bhamo is a rugged mass of hills ranging from 1,000 to 10,000 feet, and which reach their highest point apparently north-east of the Military Police outpost of Sādon. The North Shan States which run up to our official border, lie east of Bhamo across the broad Shweli valley, and are mostly of the nature of elevated undulating plateaux at a general height of 2,000 to 3,000 feet, seamed here and there by mountain ranges starting from Thibet and running southwards, which split up and run into one another, sinking gradually down to the Irrawadi and Salween valleys to the west and east respectively. Loi Ling, the highest mountain mass in this area, attains 8,840 feet; while several other peaks are between 6,000 and 7,000 feet high. Across the Salween the country is much less open, and consists of confused masses of intricate hills. In all this area the rainy season may be said to commence late in April, and to continue off and on till August, usually the wettest month; the annual rainfall varying between sixty inches in the more open country to one hundred in the higher ranges. Such then is the character of our north-east frontier as carried on beyond the limit of Assam until French Indo-China territory is reached on the Mekhong river. Of all the tribes dwelling along these borders, the most numerous, powerful, and interesting are, taking them as met with going from Assam eastwards, the Kachins (Chingpaw) and Shans (Tai). But in considering these we will begin with the latter as they, from the ethnological point of view, arrived in upper Burma first.

The Shan, or Tai race of Indo-Siamese origin at

present is the most widespread and numerous in the Indo-Chinese Peninsula, being found from Assam to Bankok and well into the Chinese Provinces of Yūnnan and Kwangsi. The cradle of this, as with all the races in the Indo-Chinese Peninsula, is the region of the head waters of the Irrawadi and other great rivers in the mountainous region of north-eastern Thibet,

A SHAN MAN.

whence successive waves of emigration have populated the country far to the south. A French savant, M. Terrien, places this race cradle in the Kiunlung mountains north of Ssu-chuan, and is of opinion the Shan migration began towards Siam about the end of the fifth or beginning of the sixth century A.D., and that their earliest settlements lay in the Shweli valley east of Bhamo. It is generally believed the Tai peoples migrated first in the far-off past, and, taking a westerly trend, occupied Siam and the country to the south of it. Certain it is that they followed up this migration by one later, when they trekked west across the Mekhong and Salween, gradually occupying upper Burma until an outlying portion of this wave of advance reached Hkāmti Lông, which was then inhabited only by a weak Kachin tribe, the first party of one of the great Kachin migrations which had begun to move south from north-eastern Thibet. The Tai race gradually consolidated a strong kingdom between the upper Irrawadi and upper Chindwyn, known in early times as that of Pông, the capital of which still remains in the present town of Mogoung. But in the long period of time, before the Pông kingdom could make itself felt, the Kachins were increasing in numbers in Hkāmti Lông, and in course of time expanded across the Patkoi range and down the Hukong valley, driving the Tai (Shan) peoples before them, and so isolating the early Shan colony in Kkāmti Lông, which explains the presence of this interesting and somewhat cultivated section so far from its brethren and now surrounded by other peoples. The increasing power of the Shans of Pông, however, arrested the advance of the Kachins and thrust them back, not in the direction whence they had come, but in the direction of the Mali-kha river.

Siam is said to have become a kingdom in the very early part of the fourteenth century, and previous to this no authentic history of this people exists, nothing but fabulous tales and legends ; though here and there ancient Chinese chronicles refer to the growing strength of this people. That they had settled forms of government is shown by the Pông kingdom which existed long previous to the fourteenth century, and is proved by Captain Pemberton's discovery in 1835 at Manipur of an old Shan chronicle which, on translation, was found to contain interesting records of Shan doings at Mogoung. It was from this kingdom that, in the beginning of the thirteenth century, Chukapha, the Tai ruler, invaded Assam, subduing various tribes and establishing the Ahom dynasty, which we have seen in the history of that province was for six centuries almost the dominant power in that part of India. According to Burman chronicles, the earliest invasion of Wesāli Lông, as they called Assam, was in the middle of the twelfth century, when a Tai king, Samlungpha, marched an army of 900,000 across the Patkoi, received the submission unopposed of the Assam ministers, and returned. This, however, is most improbable, although the Burmese national era, and with it more or less regular records began about 638 A.D., as the Ahoms themselves make no mention of any earlier western trek than that which occurred in the thirteenth century. But long before either the Pông or Siamese kingdoms made themselves known, the Shans had made an earlier State for themselves in southern China, namely, that of Nānchao (or Tālifu) which, according to Chinese chronicles unravelled by Mr. Parker, was very powerful and quite independent until the Mongol invasion of Kublai Khan in 1253 A.D. This Nānchao kingdom appears to have been most extensive touching Maghada (Bengal) on the west, Thibet on the north, and Cambodia on the south, which latter State the chronicles allude to as "the Female Prince State," as a queen of that country married an Indian adventurer who came from Cambōd in western India, and gave the name of his original home to his new country.

From Parker's translation we learn that the Shans in Nānchao were powerful and well organised, and although Chinese history maintains they formed part of their empire, yet it is certain that they were an

SHAN TRADERS.

independent community with ministers of state, record officers, officers of commerce, and an army with its usual departments. This all ceased to exist when they were no longer a conquering power, which began to come about in the middle of the eleventh century; and when the Chinese forces, after many efforts, succeeded in splitting the Nānchao kingdom in two taking the northern part, of which Tālifu was the most important city. The southern part, left to itself, spread and acquired supremacy over Siam and Burma;

until in our own times, with the exception of their Siamese brethren, the Shans deteriorated and came successively under Chinese, then Burmese, and finally English rule.

The first definite capital the Shans possessed in upper Burma is said by Mr. Ney Elias to have been Cheila, now the modern Selān, on the Shweli valley to the north-west of the present North Shan States. Selān is now a village of no great size, but has signs of a bygone importance. It stands on the highest part of an irregular shaped plateau 200 to 300 feet above the Shweli, and this plateau is completely surrounded by an entrenched ditch, in many places forty to fifty feet deep. There is no doubt a wall once existed, but this has long since completely mouldered away. A few miles off across the Shweli is Pang Hkan, also another old city with remains of an earth parapet and ditch enclosing a large area. Burmese history is silent with regard to this particular Shan power, but Tai chronicles indicate that it was probably in fair prosperity about the ninth century; while Mr. S. W. Cocks, in his work on Burma, goes so far as to state the Shan rule was practically supreme in Burma with the exception of Arrakan, by the beginning of the fourteenth century. By the middle of the fifteenth century the Burmese, however, had established their authority over the Shans, which condition having lasted one hundred years, was upset by the Shans of Mogoung, who revolted so successfully that they conquered the Burmese and practically reigned at Ava some thirty odd years.

Mogoung bears even now every evidence of having once been a large and thriving centre in which can be seen long stretches of paved streets, while the entire surrounding country for scores of miles bears traces of well-used roads and ruins of substantial bridges. But wars with the Burmese in the seventeenth and eighteenth centuries, and finally its sack by the Kachins, in 1883, brought about its ruin; which, but for the advent of the British, would have been permanent.

As in Assam, so in upper Burma, devastating wars had led in the past to the entire depopulation of once

ANCIENT "VALLUM" AND GATEWAY IN MOGOUNG DISTRICT.

thriving tracts of country, and the luxuriant forest growths have covered and obliterated almost all traces of towns and forts. Here and there in the depth of almost primeval forest one may come upon a "vallum" on which stand trees of fifteen feet girth and more; this may often enclose a space from one half to two miles square, round the outside of which can be traced the moat, often fifteen feet or more across and ten feet deep, but now filled with vegetation and cane break instead of water. The mouldering ramparts are sometimes found to be ten to twenty feet high, and must have engaged the labour of a host through several years to build up. Here and there a tumulus may be found covered by pipal trees and the earth of white ants.

The Shans have now become largely assimilated to the Burmese, their dress and even language is going; while their written character, being less and less used, will soon disappear, except perhaps in the Hkāmti Lông country. Shans are found for more than one hundred miles north of Mogoung, as also in the Hukong and Tanai valleys, the latter being the name of the chief source of the Chindwyn river. They are now great traders, though usually on a small scale as they lack capital; but of late years, with the opening of roads and railways and the general safety of the same, the volume of traffic which consists in the main of pickled and dried tea, bullocks, ponies, hides and horn, sugar, potatoes, and lac, has greatly increased. Shans almost always surround their villages with bamboo or fruit and flowering trees, giving them an appearance of comfort and beauty. They bury their dead in groves near the village or out in the jungle. The Chinese Shans dress almost invariably in indigo blue clothes, while British Shans adopt white, and their women incline to copy the Burmese, using, to quote a certain writer, "a panel variation in adornment of the identical seductive garment doubtless invented by some Burmese coquette." The chief distinction seems to lie in the different ways in which Chinese or British Shan women wear their turbans. Chinese Shans seemed to have preserved their language far more than the

Group of Shans and Palaungs.

rest of their clans, their chiefs only speaking Chinese. These people as a race are in appearance much the same as Burmese or Siamese, but are generally fairer. They are muscular and well formed and dress in short trousers (bounbees) and a jacket. With the well-to-do men the trousers are voluminous and the fork so low down as to look more like a skirt. A great broad-brimmed, close-woven grass hat is much worn by the British Shans, while his Chinese confrère uses a blue turban. Their chief national weapon is a long, slightly curved, sharp-pointed sword. Shan women are fair, but lack in face and dress the good looks and coquetry of their Burmese sisters. They are a quiet, mild, good-humoured race, and temperate in their habits as regards the use of alcohol and opium. Their religion is now everywhere Buddhist, though in ancient times, when the Nānchao kingdom flourished, they were mostly worshippers of spirits, dragons, and the dead. At one time it is certain the worship of Shiva obtained a hold over the more western Shans, and according to old legends, Buddhism in a debased form was gradually established after 500 A.D., until, by the middle of the sixteenth century it had gained ground in a purer form amongst all those who were in closer contact with Burma. But even now there is a strong animistic tendency among the Shans in British territory. With them still each day has its presiding Nāt or spirit, who requires a particular diet on certain days, different as the moon waxes or wanes. With the Shans also monks attend death-beds purely with the idea of keeping away demons, and not with the view of religious help to the departing person.

CHAPTER XIII

THE KACHINS

THIS strong and widely scattered tribe, called in Burma "Chingpaw," and in Assam known as "Singphos" (the meaning of each being simply "men") were almost the first of the frontier people the British came in contact with in upper Burma after the annexation in 1885. Colonel Hannay of the Assam Light Infantry, who was an acknowledged authority on these people, says, "Their territories are bounded on the east and south-east by Yünnan, the western part of which they have now overrun, on the west by Assam, south by the 24th degree N. longitude roughly, while of their northern limits which come in contact with the Khunnongs to whom they are allied we know little or nothing."

Their northern regions are inaccessible and explorations almost impossible. Generally, then, they may be said to inhabit the country lying north-north-west, and north-east of upper Burma, and during the last seventy years have been spreading further south into the North Shan States and to Bhamo and Katha—a procedure which our advent into upper Burma put a period to.

The Kachins are broken up into small communities, each under its own chief; which arrangement, as it gave no central authority to be dealt with, produced for the British no end of trouble for some years, each little clan raiding or submitting as it felt disposed. They are essentially a hill-dwelling people, though their cultivation is often low down in the plains, and they divide themselves into two great political divisions, namely, the Kamsa Kachins who have rulers, and the Kumlao Kachins who have none, and but rarely even assemble village councils. There is also a sort of national division of Kachins into "Khākus," or Northerners, living between the Mali-kha and Nmai-kha rivers above the Confluence, and the "Ching-paw," or southerners, who migrated furthest from the ancestral home in the mountains of north-east Thibet.

We have seen how the first migration of these people led them in a small community into what is now the Hkāmti country; whence, on receiving a fresh influx of immigrants, they expanded across the Patkoi, pushing back the Shans in those regions until the latter, gaining strength in the Pông kingdom, were in their turn able to thrust the Kachins back but in the direction of the Mali-kha river, where they were forced to live until the dissolution of the Shan kingdom towards the end of the thirteenth century, when the Kachins again set themselves in motion, migrating south and south-east. During all this period another migratory wave of what are now spoken of as Thibeto-Burmans was gradually advancing down the Nmai-kha valley further east, and these eventually met the western stream in the neighbourhood of Myitkhyina and Mogoung, where they became powerful, ousting the Shans, and overaweing them and the Burmans to such an extent that it was the usual habit of the latter in the riverine tracts to sleep in their boats on the rivers, that they might have some chance of escape from the sudden raids the Kachins constantly

KACHIN GIRL

indulged in. It is not necessary to dive into the bewildering mass of tribelets into which this race is split up ; a look into the Gazetteer of Upper Burma will satisfy those who need deeper detail on the subject ; so it will suffice for this history to deal with the five parent tribes only, and two or three others of the more important "Cognate tribes," as they are called; and who, though descending it is thought from the same common ancestors, have evolved certain widely different manners, habits, and even languages, from those of the true Kachins.

These parent tribes are :—

(1) The Marips, who dwell west of the Mali-kha river near the Hukong valley round the Jade mine area, and to the west of the Indawgyi lake. They are a powerful tribe, and one that has always been the most friendly disposed towards British authority. Of these there are fifteen sub-tribes.

(2) The Lahtaungs, who apparently first dwelt in the area enclosed by the Mali-kha and Nmai-kha rivers, but some distance above the Confluence. They have now, however, spread southwards till they reach the upper defile of the Irrawadi river, and extend into parts of the North Shan hills. This tribe is split up into eighteen sub-divisions, of which only one the Sana Lahtaungs, were openly hostile to British rule, giving cause for various columns to move against them up to 1896. They dwell now mostly west of the Irrawadi and north of Mogoung; and it was this sub-division that made the well-known and successful raid on Myitkhyina in December, 1892, when they burnt the court-house and civil officers' residences, and generally caused a stampede of all who were then in Myitkhyina, together with some of the Mogoung Levy in garrison there.

(3) The Lepais are said to be the largest and most powerful of the Kachin tribes and are found in the country north and north-east of Mogoung, around

Myitkhyina and away into the Pang Hkan hills south-east of Bhamo. Some are also found scattered in the North Shan hills. They are divided up into seventeen sub-divisions, of whom only two are worth noticing here, namely, the Thamā section, whose

KACHIN MEN (MOGOUNG).

hostility in 1889 necessitated a punitive force being sent against them, when 329 of their houses were burnt, 124,000 lbs. of paddy destroyed, and many killed before they submitted two years later ; and the Kaori section who, occupying the hills east and south-east of Bhamo dominate the main route for traffic with China, and are rather notorious robbers. Of the other Lepai section, the most troublesome have been the Szi about Mogoung, the Hpankan south-east of Bhamo, and the Lakhum east of Bhamo along the right bank of the Shweli river, against whom in 1886 to 1892 various punitive expeditions had to be sent before their final submission. Of all the Kachin peoples these Lepais have shown the most hostility in the early years after the annexation.

(4) The N'khums, who dwell in the region south of Hkāmti Lông and west of the Mali-kha river with a few scattered villages along the frontier and in the North Shan States.

(5) The Marans who are found all along the border in scattered communities in the country about the Amber mines and west of the Mali-kha. Both these latter tribes appear to have given little or no trouble in the past, and have no particular interest. Of the so-called "Cognate tribes," who, though of the same stock as Kachins, are yet different in habits and speech, the most noticeable are the Mārus, Lashis, Yawyins or Lihsaws, and Khunongs.

The first-named are found chiefly on the border-land between Burma and China, east of Loi Nju, near the Confluence, and up the Nmai-kha river. They are also met with in North Hsen Wi district in the Shan hills, and even down in the Katha district. They have no sub-tribes, but every village has its own chief, and these are not always at peace with each other. They are also great slave traders. Lieutenant Pottinger, R.A., who has travelled a good deal amongst these people, says those living along the border-land are an undersized folk of poor physique, though with more pleasing faces than are usually possessed by Kachins. The further north one goes the finer does the tribe become, until the Nanwu Mārus are reached—fine sturdy men with powerful limbs and generally splendid physique.

The Lashis appear to be confined to the Chinese border north, north-east, and east of Bhamo, and appear to be allied to the Mārus. During 1891–92 they came into collision with the British troops.

The Yawyins, or Lihsaws, are not true Chingpaw (Kachin), as shown by their language, which is entirely different. They are found chiefly in the vicinity of Sadon and scattered throughout the higher ranges of the North Shan States. Usually a bigger set of people than the Kachins, they are interesting as being closely allied to the Muhsös, or Lāhus, as the Shans call them, amongst whom Prince Henri d'Orléans travelled, and who are said formerly to have been powerful even to possessing a kingdom in the neighbourhood of east Thibet, where the great rivers rise which eventually descend into Yünnan and Burma, *vide* Colborne Baber's and Cooper's writings on the subject, who about 1875 and 1877 got through from Yünnan to Ta-chien-loo on the eastern Thibet border, and through Ssü-chuan to Bathang, respectively. The Khunongs are found east of Hkāmti Lông (or Bor Hkāmti) and appear to touch even the Salween river. An old Shan chronicle mentions them as being one of the important races which assisted in forming the Pông kingdom (Mogoung); and Mr. Ney Elias, one of the great authorities on these little-known peoples, finds a very close kinship between them and the Mishmis of Assam. General Woodthorpe states their language resembles that of the Singphos (Chingpaw), and alludes to them as a small-statured folk, fair and pleasant of face, timid of disposition, and consequently much oppressed by the Singphos on the south and Hkāmti Shans on the west, to whom they pay tribute.

They trade with the Chinese, Burmans, and also with the Lamas of Thibet; and their most valuable possessions are the silver mines of Nogmung east of the Nam Tisang, which were visited by the late General Macgregor, who describes their rude methods of extracting and melting the ore in iron vessels over red-hot charcoal, a draught being kept up by blow-pipes on opposite sides, and the melted silver run off in iron pipes. The Khunongs never live in large villages, their houses are usually scattered over the hills in pairs, more often singly. The tribe is said to pay tribute to the Hkāmtis, and to do a considerable amount of house building and agriculture for them, and to be also subject to their more northern neighbours the Khenungs, of whom very little is known, and who again come under China. The Khunongs do a considerable trade in gold and beeswax, and it is said the former is plentiful in their hills. From native sources of information it is reported that extensive silver mines exist east of the Nmai-kha river.

Further south in the Kachin country, namely, between the Hukong valley and Mogoung lie the Amber and Jade mine districts which produce quantities of these valuable commodities. The amber is found on a small range in the south-west corner of the Hukong valley near and to the south of Mayankwān village.

The actual mines are pits often nearly fifty fathoms deep sunk in the hard blue clay in which the resin is found in small flat blocks up to one foot long by six inches thick. This trade is chiefly with China, as is also that of jade which is found in the country about Kāmaing, north-west of Mogoung, and to a certain extent in the Katha district further south. It is found in certain valleys in the form of large boulders, though here and there it is dug out of hill sides at

CANE BRIDGE IN THE KACHIN COUNTRY.

a considerable elevation. These boulders are split by heating, and the jade stone in the centre then chipped out very carefully. This industry partakes of the nature of a pure gamble, for it is impossible to tell with any accuracy how much or in what quality jade exists in any boulder. All these tribes differ in appearance, habits, and dialects, and all writers say those whose habitat lies further north are the finer specimens of humanity. Although amongst them are to be found various shades of complexion and shapes of face, yet there can be no doubt as to the origin of the Kachins, which was Tartar, and their original home the region south of the Great Gobi desert, whence migration started southwards. Their religion in general is that of spirit worship and the propitiation of malevolent demons; while their marriage ceremonies usually partake of the nature of abduction, which, among the wealthier households is merely nominal in form, but is actually carried out among the common folk. Their morals, from our point of view may be considered somewhat lax, which is the case with all their neighbours right away to Assam, as young people are allowed to consort together as they please before marriage. If they do not care for each other they separate, and each is free to experiment with someone else. Should they so care, they marry: and Kachins claim that this arrangement does away with the chances of lapses in chastity and consequent trouble thereby after marriage. Should a child inopportunely arrive as a result of these intimacies, the man almost invariably marries the girl or has to pay a heavy fine to her parents.

Kachins bury their dead with a certain amount of ceremony in timber coffins, offerings of pig and libations of rice beer being made to the spirits. The Mārus are the only Kachin people who burn their dead and bury the ashes.

The weapons of all Kachins and Shans are fairly similar, namely, cross-bows, spears and dahs, while amongst those in touch with Burma and China muzzle-loading guns are also found, and even Winchester carbines obtained from Yünnan. Old Tower

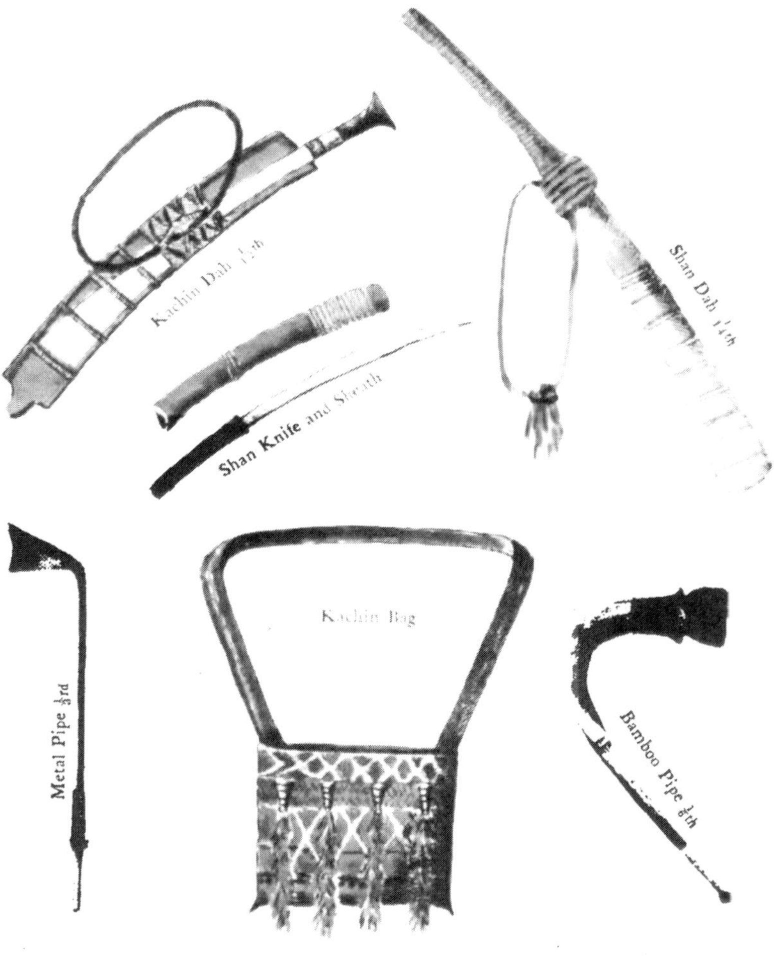

SHAN AND KACHIN WEAPONS, ETC.

flintlocks of 1800 are often met with, and a few of the more powerful chiefs used to own jingals and swivel guns; but these are a rarity nowadays. They make their own coarse powder and use iron bullets and slugs. The dahs used by all Kachins and Hkāmti Shans north of the Confluence are made by the small Tāreng tribe, who are distinct from the Kachins, whose habitat is north of Hkāmti Lông, and who are called by Mr. Errol Gray "the blacksmiths of the Khākus" (North Kachins). The metal is very durable, and the dahs are made in four varieties, of which the so-called "streaked" variety is used only by the upper classes. The Kachin dah, their national weapon, is about eighteen inches long, and differs from that of the Shans or Burmans in its curious wooden half sheath in which lies the weapon, one and a half inches wide at the hilt, increasing to two and a half inches at the truncated tip. The back is slightly curved, and the whole weapon wonderfully well balanced. It is used only for cutting, unlike the Shan weapon which is sharp-pointed for thrusting.

Up to the arrival of the British on the scene, the Kachins were inveterate slave traders, which national custom was kept up by constant raids. Their ideas of war, like those of the Shans and other tribes, are chiefly those of sudden raids, and with few exceptions during our troubles with them after the annexation of upper Burma, they have acted on the defensive, planning their stockades and earthworks with rapidity and skill. The ground in front and flanks of these they stud with "pānjis" (bamboo spikes hardened in fire) varying from a few inches to four feet long. Being hidden in long grass these are difficult to see, and men running on to them get severe and often fatal wounds. Pitfalls three feet deep "pānjied" at the bottom and neatly covered over are also frequently used. Favourite spots for the defence of their villages, which generally straggle among the hills with primeval forest all around, are usually found in thick jungle, ravines with steep approaches, or river gorges, where the Kachins will block and spike the approaches at suitable spots and have their guns trained on this ground from above or from the opposite side of the gorge, to open on the enemy when brought to a halt by the obstruction. As a result of many difficulties and losses when at first British troops were confronted by these Kachin tactics, the following plan was invariably adopted: an advance guard of six men leads, two flanking parties follow at some distance, for in these wooded regions troops are absolutely confined to the one path or track, and with the latter is a mountain gun. As soon as the advance guard comes on to the stockade or obstruction, word is passed back and this party disappears into the jungle at the side. The flanking parties work at once round each side of the defences, while the gun is pushed forward to a convenient spot and used against the works, and the main body then advances. When Kachins attack they do so at night, preferably just before moonrise. They are not head-hunters like their western brethren, the Nagas of Assam, but cut off the head of an enemy in proof that the Kachin brave has killed his man; they then throw the head away as having no further value.

In character these people are said by all who have come in contact with them to be vindictive and treacherous; but no doubt there are good points in them which careful fostering may bring out. For instance, they have been tried in certain Military Police Battalions, and those who have had command of them speak well of their soldierly qualities and the readiness with which they come under our notions of discipline, etc. In 1898 they came under fire for the first time and acquitted themselves in a praiseworthy manner.

Myitkhyina, the important and most northerly of our frontier stations in the Kachin country, is on the Irrawadi some 1,400 miles from its mouth, and in fairly close contact with the Chinese borderland which is guarded by the strong outposts east of the river of Simā, Sadōn, Seneku, Htagaw, and to which Hpimaw has recently been added; all of which are in helio communication with Myitkhyina. It lies in a broad, well-watered plain, and is now a model cantonment well laid out, with good roads, comfortable bungalows, and well-built lines for a strong Military Police Battalion of Goorkhas, who furnish the outposts and keep watch and ward over the wild tract of little-known country which has frequently been a source of trouble either of raids, smuggling, or demarcation difficulties. Myitkhyina in its early days suffered some vicissitudes, and at one time was so badly raided by Kachins (1893) that an undignified stampede of all in the place occurred, who fell back on Bhamo. It is now connected with the outer world by railway to Mandalay and Rangoon.

Palaungs, Wās, and Panthays.

A description of the border people of upper Burma would be incomplete without some reference to these tribes, who are separate races dwelling in and along our north-east boundaries. The Palaungs have a State of their own, called by the Shans "Tawngpeng," and being a quiet, peaceful folk, have not come much into notice. They usually inhabit the higher hills in both British and Chinese Shan country, and are great cultivators of tea. Ethnological savants differ considerably as to their original stock, one connecting them with Môn or Talaing, another with Cambōdian origin. From their own legends they would appear to have been in Tawngpeng long before the downfall of the ancient Shan kingdom of Nānchao about the middle of the ninth century. They are an uncouth-looking but industrious race, are keen Buddhists, but also keep up a belief in spirits, whom they worship in trees, hills, and rocks. The Chinese pagoda on Loi Hpra, for instance, is worshipped by them, as also a very large old tea tree at Loi Seng which was planted 160 years ago. The men have now almost entirely adopted the Shan attire, while their women still keep up their own tribal distinction in their dresses which are bright in colour, consisting of a little dark blue jacket, a coloured skirt and blue trousers; and on the head a large hood brought to a point behind the head and reaching down over the shoulders, the ends of which have white borders with ornamental bits of scarlet, blue, and black velvet worked in. The skirts having panels of various colours let in, the whole attire forms a pleasingly gay effect when seen on gala and festive occasions. Although both Palaungs and the Wā disclaim all connection with each other, their languages have shown conclusively that they must have had some common origin. The second tribe, namely, the Wā, state they are a race quite apart

A PALAUNG GIRL.

from the Palaungs and others, and are divided by us into wild and tame Wās—the former living in a compact block of country beyond our north-eastern frontier running for one hundred miles or so along the Salween and between that river and the Mekhong, the boundary of French influence, the latter dwelling inside our border line. They are a savage and treacherous race, and till visited by a British party in 1893, had always enjoyed the reputation of being cannibals, which is not the case. They are, however, notorious head-hunters, not with the view of success amongst the fair sex (as with the Nagas), nor do they seem to regard heads as warlike tokens, but rather in the light of protection against evil spirits—without a skull his crops would fail or cattle die. The heads are set up on posts under the avenue of trees by which the villages are approached, and sometimes can be counted by hundreds on either side of these avenues. It is said they have a tariff for heads, those more dangerous to obtain, such as a Chinaman's, being valued at Rs. 50, but the general rate is from Rs. 2 to Rs. 10. Their villages, unlike those of the Kachins, are built on bare open hill sides visible for miles, the only trees in the immediate vicinity being those of the stately, sombre avenues of approach. When heads are brought home after a raid a great drinking bout with singing and dancing takes place, while the war drum, a huge tree trunk hollowed out, leaving only a narrow strip for the sound to emerge from, is frantically beaten. These drums, like those of the northern Nagas, in Assam, give out a deep, vibrating sound which travels a great distance, and are only beaten at times of crisis or of importance in the community. In time of tribal warfare a Wā village, and these are often of remarkable size, may be said to be almost impregnable. They stand high on hill slopes and are surrounded by an earth rampart six to eight feet high, which is overgrown with a dense covering of thorn bushes and cactus, while outside this again is a very deep ditch also concealed by shrubs and grass. The only entrance is through a long sunken road often covered to form a sort of tunnel which is made to wind, so as to obviate the possibility of an enemy firing up it. In time of danger these approaches are sown with bamboo spikes (pānjies), the whole forming a defence most difficult to get through. The Wās grow a considerable amount of opium, which at great profit to themselves is taken by Shans and Chinese. They are also heavy drinkers of a strong spirit made from rice, and are good agriculturists. Their dress is conspicuous in both sexes by its scantiness and unattractiveness. In hot weather neither wears anything except on occasions of ceremony, the men then simply wearing a strip of cotton cloth passed between the legs and tied round the waist so that the small tassled ends hang down in front. The women's only garment is a short petticoat falling down from the hips for a few inches only, made of coarse cotton. But as the women are fair, shapely, and decidedly pretty, perhaps scantiness of attire is the less to be regretted. As for religion, theirs is mostly that of spirit worship, though a few profess to be Buddhists. They bury their dead in the village in front of the deceased's house with all his personal ornaments. One writer on these people states that in spite of their head-hunting propensities which arise from a mistaken agricultural theory, the fear of evil spirits, and not from ferocity, they are a brave, independent, energetic, and industrious lot; while other tribes affirm that the Wās are not bad neighbours.

North of the Wās, and between them and China proper, come the Lolos and Muhsös or Lāhus, tribes of whom but little is known, and only a few scattered communities of the latter dwell in the Northern Shan States, namely, in Hsen Wi and Hsipaw. The Muhsös are said to be a warlike tribe, and it is known the Chinese of Yünnan have frequently been in conflict with them, and were only subdued as late as 1887, when a Chinese General found it necessary to use Krupp guns against them. They are very expert cross-bowmen, and their arrows are often poisoned. Prince Henri d'Orléans travelled through their country in 1895, and speaks of them as having been at one time Buddhists, though now they have mostly reverted to their old spirit worship. He also states they have a written character not unlike Chinese, and assumes the Lolos and Muhsös to be practically the same tribe.

The Lolos occupy country in south Ssü-chuan, near the Ssü-chuan and Yünnan border, and are described as a tall, energetic race. They mix a great deal with the Chinese, and have a written character resembling that called Indo-Pali, having its origin in picture-writing. They burn their dead, and have a curious form of religion based on a belief in a future state of retribution. In a few cases only have Lolos adopted Buddhism. Mr. Hosie, who in 1883 journeyed from Chengtu, the capital of Ssü-chuan to Yünnanfu, passed through their country, and records the number of Chinese garrisons in mud forts in the valleys to control this people, while the hill country is left severely alone by them. In fact, the Lolos, who appeared a warlike, truculent race and are continually raiding, were distinctly held in dread by the Chinese. From the strongly stockaded Chinese outposts and guard-houses, everything pointed to being in a dangerous locality, and parties of Celestial soldiery armed with old muskets, swords, and halberts, escorted him through the Lolo country for days. In his travels through this country and southern Yünnan, Prince Henri d'Orléans speaks of the seasons wet or dry being far less marked than in the country further south and nearer Burma. The climate of the upper Mekhong appears very dry, even in the summer there is a very small rainfall only. This changes again further north, where in the neighbourhood of Attentze and Ouisifu, two rainy seasons occur, namely, July to September and again in February, the latter being the heavier. The Salween valley, being covered with dense vegetation, is far damper than that of the Mekhong, and in the upper Irrawadi basin he says the two seasons are well marked, and the summer rains are abundant. Here in winter they noticed a remarkable and continuous absence of wind, a condition obtaining nowhere else in their long journey from Tonkin to Assam. Except on the peaks of Likiang, Dokerla, and Pemachou, there appeared to be no perennial snow in this part of western Yünnan, but the party found the ranges dividing the Mekhong, Salween, and Irrawadi, and the Mekhong from the Yiang-tse-kiang, to be deep in snow from December to May, and no crossings are feasible then. He also states that in winter it is impossible to cross from the Mekhong to the Salween further north than Lao or Fey-long-kiao, which lie a little west of Talifu.

This tally of Upper Burman border tribes would be incomplete without reference to the Panthays, whose chief settlement on our side of the frontier is at Pan Lông in the North Shan State of Sön-mu. Their proper habitat is, however, south of Talifu and also in Momein (Tengyueh), and they are known to us as being traders and muleteers on the different trade routes between southern China and Burma. They are Mahomedans, and are descendants of Mahomedan military emigrants who settled in far-off times and married Chinese wives. Mahomedanism reached China through the more eastern conquests of Tamerlane, when numbers of his soldiery remained behind in the Chinese provinces of Kānsu and Yünnan. The Panthays are a fine and not unwarlike race, as their conflicts with the Chinese in the last seventy years go to show; who only crushed out the rebellion by a series of ruthless massacres of the Panthays, which chroniclers state cost seven millions of lives between Chinese weapons and the plague, which disease broke out in the decimated region, spread in 1893 to Hong Kong, and three years later to Bombay.

All this part of our borderland, where Shans, Panthays, and Palaungs are met with, has attracted all who have made acquaintance with it—its hills and valleys, woods and plains, picturesque peoples, affording constant change to the mind and delight to the eye. The writer in 1901 travelled across from the Naga hills and reached the Irrawadi at Katha, and the scenes and interests impressed themselves on him greatly so that possibly a part of his wanderings about the Bhamo border may interest others. At Katha he was once more in reach of civilised methods of travelling, and on a comfortable steamer journeying up river, passing Shwegu, noted justly (from what he saw) for the good looks of its ladies, and Thūnyaw Island, where large fairs are held, and immense numbers of delicately shaped white pagodas stand out amongst the general greenery. The lower Defile, seven and a half miles long, was entered at daybreak, and here the hills rise straight from the river's edge, which in one place narrows from 700 to 250 yards across. The entrance to the Defile, with a little golden pagoda built some way up a tremendous precipice, is particularly striking. At Bhamo, which, it is interesting to know, held in the latter part of the eighteenth century an English factory, of which the brick ruins in old Bhamo, near the Taping river, are still pointed out, he found he was in time to join in with Captain L. of the Military Police Battalion, who was going out seventy miles east on to the Chinese border to locate a new outpost. His company of Sikhs had gone ahead a few days, so we followed, riding thirteen miles to Mānsi at the foot of the hills, and thence seventeen miles up hill, along a vile road through dense forest to Warraboon at the top of the range. The rains were just over, and traders were beginning to trek down to Bhamo from China and the Shan States, and the road every now and then would be blocked by droves of Shan cattle or Panthay mules with their loads of merchandise carried on peculiar-shaped pack saddles which are not fastened on to the animals as ours would be, but keep position by balance. The loads are very easily and quickly lifted on and off, and no sore backs were noticed. The leading animals in these droves had most musical bells attached to their head-gear, which echoed through the forest and along the hill sides in a most attractive manner. Down below in Bhamo it was still hot and stuffy, but Warraboon at 4,400 feet was distinctly and pleasantly cold, and the evening view over the Irrawadi from an open spur near a Kachin rest-house in which we spent the night was exceedingly fine. The next day the road followed the top of the range for some miles till the small bamboo rest-house at Nāmkai was reached, in which we rested and tiffined. The hill sides about here at this season were covered with a creeper, whose masses of close white blossoms gave the appearance of a heavy fall of snow. Far off, and below, a glimpse was obtained of the Shweli valley backed by the distant blue mountains of the Shan States and China. That evening Pungkan was reached, and we found a small two-roomed grass and bamboo "bāshā" had been run up for us by the Sikhs who had arrived and had hutted themselves in rows of similar shelters on an open stretch of grass land a little south of the village and close to the border, which here is the Namwān stream. The next two days were spent in selecting an advantageous site for the new outpost, in pegging out the traces for its earthwork defences, and in fishing the neighbouring stream, but with indifferent success. The weather was now glorious and the views delightful, especially about evening, while at that time the chimes from the different Shan monasteries added to one's pleasure. The first evening there will not be easily forgotten. We were lounging and smoking by our small hut, near by the Sepoys preparing their evening meals, and to our front long stretches of turf land sloping gently down to the Shweli river six miles off and rolling through richly cultivated country, beyond the mountains of south-west China, with the last glow of sunset lingering on them. To our left and one and a half miles away, a long wooded spur dipping into the main valley, and at its lower end a picturesque Chinese fort (Loieng), Pungkan village lying about mid-way between it and our hut. We were talking of the extreme beauty of the view, the shadows lengthen, the sunlight fades on the scene, when suddenly a burst of most glorious bell music rises from the Pungkan monastery and floats across to us; we sit up and listen intently, the chimes rise and fall, swelling, mysterious, touching music; two far-off monasteries take it up faintly, and before we realised it, the glorious sounds had ceased, a heavy silence succeeded, and both of us agreed it was most beautiful but all too short. Our third day in these parts was spent in a visit to the great fair at Namkwam, ten miles across the main valley. An early start was made, and also an unsuccessful stalk after geese on the river, but the birds were too wary. This fair was on a very large scale on the outskirts of a moderate sized town, where many years ago we had had an outpost. Lines and lines of booths were crowded with thousands of wild, strange types of humanity —Burmese, Chinese, Shans, Kachins, and Yawyins, their women with scanty coloured skirts, heavy cane gartering and marvellous hair arrangements; and Palaungs, whose ladies encircle their sturdy waists with endless coils of cane, wear silk trouserines, and carry a heavy knife sticking in their girdle. All sorts of curios and weapons could be picked up here, as well as good silk and the pretty home-made cloths beloved and distinctive of the different tribes. But even here many stalls displayed tawdry Birmingham and Manchester goods and cheap American cigarettes in thousands! Mixed up with these were quite inviting confectioners, whose refreshment stalls were always crowded; while here and there one stumbled across the same old game—the three-card trick, or thimbles and peas—always presided over by an acute-looking old Chinaman who in every case seemed to be doing a roaring trade. Not far off was the cattle fair with large numbers of excellent little Shan ponies, mules, and cows picketed in long lines for sale. Towards noon the Tsawba (chief), hearing of our presence, sent word hoping we would rest and spend the heat of the day in his house, which we gladly did—eating our tiffin in what I suppose might have been called his audience hall, a fine, large, airy timber structure, raised off the ground on piles, with a large number of spears, dahs, and old muskets ranged round the walls. The illustrious host, together with his notables, sat quietly round watching us eat with evident interest; but conversation languished, for our only interpreter knew very little Hindustani. Before leaving we persuaded our host to let us see and photo him in all his silken finery, and a very attractive group he and his two senior officials made. With this a most delightful border outing came to an end, and Bhamo was reached again three days later.

CHAPTER XIV

THE NAGA TRIBES

THE successful attack in February, 1913, of the Trans-Dikku Nagas on a column of Military Police has turned a certain amount of attention to the tribes of Nagas who, though not actually living on the North Eastern Frontier, are sufficiently near to it and have a sufficiently interesting history to warrant their being included in this volume. The name by which they are now usually known, namely, Naga, has nothing whatever to do with snakes as some think, but is a corruption of the word " nanga "—naked. Of all the people in north-east Assam these are the most powerful, and have given us more persistent trouble since 1832 than any others. They inhabit the hill country south of the Brahmaputra valley from the Singphos to the North Cachar hills, and are divided into four big tribal sections—Angāmi, Sema, Aoh, Lhota—and two smaller ones—Rengma and Kaccha Nagas. Of these, the first-named have proved the most turbulent and warlike. Their origin is rather doubtful, some savants ascribing a Mongolian origin, namely, that they are an offshoot of the very earliest migration from the neighbourhood of the Kiunlung range as carried out first by the Chins,

O 2

who located themselves far to the south in the hills between the Lushais and the Irrawadi valley. Others

ANGĀMI NAGAS IN GALA ATTIRE.

in the past have thought that they can trace their origin to the Dyāks of Borneo, who in some far-off age, it is surmised, may have trekked north through

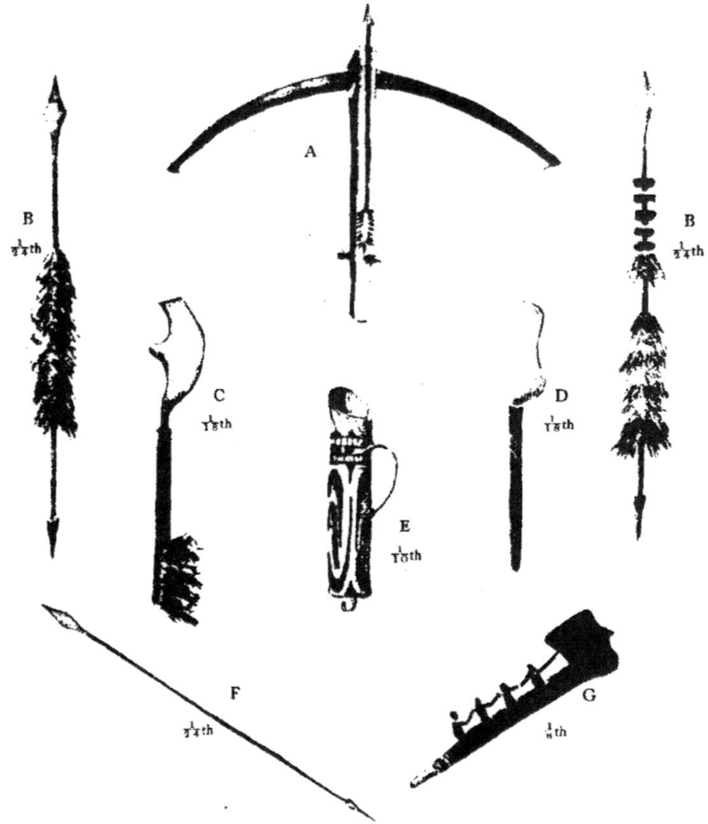

A. Cross bow used by Singphos Daphlas and Nagas on the Patkoi Range.

B. Spears used by the same with hair ornamentation. The circles denote owners rank.

C. D. Different kinds of "daos" used by the Patkoi tribes. D is double edged.

E. A bamboo drinking cup adorned with real "poker work."

F. The plain shafted spear used for throwing.

G. Carved wooden pipe used on the Western Patkoi--the bowl represents a human head, and a row of monkeys stand along the stem.

the Straits, Tenasserim, southern Burma, and Arakan, until they were brought to a standstill by either the vast walls of the Himalayas or by the southward trend of Mongolian peoples. They recognise a slight resemblance in matters of counting, names for domestic implements, in a way village architecture, and their head-hunting propensities, to those of the Dyāks; while their love for marine shells (which they part with but rarely) may seem to point to a bygone home near the sea; though now they are a far inland residing community. The late Colonel J. Johnston, formerly Political Agent at Manipur, alludes to this idea of a far southern original home for the Nagas; while the traditions of the Marām tribe of Nagas on the east of the Barail range go to show that their original home was somewhere far to the south of where they are now. It is perhaps worthy of notice that the tribe of Kukis (Lushais) with similar characteristics are still moving north; while across in Burma the great Kachin tribes have been steadily pressing south even to our day. But this old theory has practically exploded, and it is now definitely decided that this people belong to a Thibeto-Burman stock. The Nagas, particularly the Angāmis, are an athletic and by no means a bad-looking race, and are in religion spirit worshippers. They are, for savages, a moral race, the same customs in marriage obtaining with them as with the Kachins already dealt with. Their weapons are spears seven feet long and over, and short assegais which are thrown with great skill for twenty-five yards and more, a heavy battle-axe, or "dao," and at one time they possessed a considerable number of old muzzle-loading guns, which have now been gradually taken from them. Their villages are built high on the hills, strongly defended with stockades, stout walls and "pānjied"

ANGĀMI NAGAS.

ditches. The approaches to most of these are along narrow winding sunken paths, not unlike those of the Wās in Burma. All Nagas are head-hunters, their women being the chief incentive to this pursuit, as girls will not look on men with favour who have not taken heads or been in raids. Since our taking over the Naga hills this, of course, has ceased; but even of late years it has occurred that women have induced men desiring their favours to go across the border and take a head. Any are considered of value—man's, woman's, or child's—and it is curious to note that where some of the tribes adorn their shields and house fronts with rough emblems of heads taken, sometimes one will see a head represented upside down—this having been taken in pure murder. Thus do they make some slight distinction between a fairly taken head and one unfairly taken. Angāmi girls have their heads shaved clean until they marry, when they grow their hair; so that the interesting bride by her bristly pate is at once divined, with whom, as one writer puts it, "the orange blossoms of virginity are never seen by her husband." Kaccha Nagas, who are closely allied to the Angāmis and dwell just south of them, who dress similarly, and whose villages are small and houses different from their neighbours, display a tribal dress distinction only through their women, the edges of whose short, bright petticoats are embroidered with the tribal pattern. Their girls do not shave the head, but grow the hair fairly long and cut it into a deep fringe over the forehead, with rather pleasing effect. The Kaccha Nagas are a cheery and musical folk, the former quality being shown in their dances to which they are devoted and in which they are graceful performers. These dances are of a quick "heel and toe" movement, either in pairs or quartets of both sexes, and are not unlike our Highland dances. Their singing is curious—no words, and of the nature of an antiphonal chant, which is very effective.

Angāmi dances partake more of the nature of wild leaping, and they are unmusical save for a rather sad, long-drawn-out chant. The eastern Angāmis of the Kopamedza range have a most curious form of singing. A little party of young men and girls will form two separate circles, girls in one, men in the other, with a leader in the centre of each. The singing is "bouche

KACCHA NAGAS DANCING.

fermee," and one has to be close to hear well. Both circles accord with each other in the air, which is most soft and pleasing. Oddly enough, with all their warlike tendencies, the Angāmis are great traders, continually being seen in distant parts of the Assam valley, while they have been known to go even as far as Calcutta and Rangoon.

The Aoh Nagas are found from the Doyang river almost to the great bend of the Dikkoo river as it emerges from the hills into the plains, and they occupy the three ranges of hills lying between the latter river and the Assam valley. Neither this tribe nor their neighbours, the Semas, have given us very great trouble in the past, though it has been found necessary to punish for minor raids now and then, and to finally take over the countries of both tribes. Aohs are divided into two big clans—the "Chungli" and the "Mongsin." These are difficult to recog-

AOH NAGA GIRL SHOWING COIFFURE AND SHELL NECKLACE.

nise ordinarily, as the dress is the same in both; each favour certain localities, and their women denote the tribal distinction in the tattooed ornamentation of their legs from ankle to knee—one having a diamond pattern (Chungli), the other plain circles round the calf (Mongsin), both being finished off with arrow heads at the knees. The coiffure of an Aoh woman is most elaborate, the hair being coiled into a large ornate "bun" behind, which is added to with false plaits twisted in with coils of white cotton wool and with brass hair pins; the whole being supported on either side by enormous heavy brass earrings which are passed through the helix of the ear and kept in place by a string over the top of the head. Amongst the Aohs, for the preservation of order on the border, the Naga Hill Military Police Battalion have a strong outpost at Mōgōkchang (ninety-five miles north of Kohima) of a hundred rifles in an earthwork fort, and another of fifty rifles stockaded at Tamlu, forty-five miles further north-east. Both posts have good rifle ranges and drill grounds, and are rationed from Moriani and Nazira respectively, which lie in the plains, and with which they are connected by good bridle paths.

The Rengma and Lhota Nagas are uninteresting people with dirty persons and villages. The latter are chiefly noted for the very excellent domestic servants they make.

In the extreme north of the Naga hills are the Lengta Nagas, a feeble tribe allied to the strong, fighting clans of the Trans-Dikkoo country, but who are terrible opium eaters and incapable of any heavy work. They, or rather their menkind, used to go naked, but of late years they have adopted a small blue loin cloth.

The Sema Nagas are the next largest tribe to the Aohs and Angāmis, but are not quite so warlike as the latter. They are divided into two large clans, namely, the "Yepatomi," or those dwelling in the low hills about the Doyang valley, and the "Zjhūmomi" Semas, who occupy the higher ranges in the neighbourhood of the Tita and Tizoo rivers. These latter are a fine sturdy race, and have chiefs among them with real power to rule. Semas are, however, notorious thieves and drunkards. How far east they extend beyond the Tita river is at present unknown. The customs of many of these tribes are interesting and peculiar. As stated before, all marry when adults, and all girls and young men can consort openly together till marriage. Village arrangements and

SEMA NAGAS IN WAR PAINT.

architecture are different in each tribe, the Angāmis having the larger more permanently built houses, the Rengmas and Lhotas building smaller and meaner-looking dwellings, the Aohs and Lengtas again living in large villages, the individual houses being lightly built of bamboo and standing high off the ground on piles. Angāmis, Kacchas, Lhotas, and Rengmas bury in their villages, Aohs smoke dry the late lamented and then lay him on a high sort of trestle thatched over, on which they hang his ornaments and cloths and stand his weapons in front. The

Aoh Naga Graves.

trestles with the dead are placed on either side of the big shady avenues by which the villages are approached. In the rains, when dry wood is scarce and smoking a corpse long and tedious work, they are often placed on their trestles with the process only half completed ; and the passage of these avenues is then not a matter of pleasure for those of delicate nostrils. In the north of the district at Tamlu and over amongst the Trans-Dikkoo people, their dead are placed in rough-hewn log coffins, or are carefully wrapped round with leaves, which are then lodged up in big trees near the villages, the head in some clans being wrenched off and laid at the base of the tree. As wind and weather work upon the trees and coffins these are often dislodged, and the scene is then more gruesome than curious. In dress Angāmis and Aohs are the most picturesque in their war paint with short black sort of kilt or a sporran, both adorned with cowrie shells, ivory or brass armlets, cane head-dress mounting the tail feathers of the toucan, coloured cane leggings, huge white seashells worn at the back of the neck, and their daos and spears with fringes of gaily dyed hair. Aoh women wear a long blue shawl covering them entirely, while the Angāmi wears a short brightly striped petticoat and small coloured shawl with brass bangles and large necklaces of shells, coloured beads, and rough cut cornelians. Semas and Rengmas are the least attractive in attire, which is exceedingly scanty. In the north round Tamlu and at Lakma a little further east the people go nude ; the men only in the former, both sexes in the latter, and it certainly made us feel at first somewhat awkward when the 1900 expedition entered Lakma to be confronted by the villagers about their business in what Trilby called the "all together," and see men and girls chaffing each other with nothing but necklace and armlets on. East of the Angāmis come other clans who discard clothes, namely, the Sohemi folk and the Tankhul Nagas, whose ring-wearing habit has aroused much curiosity; though these latter are only actually nude in the heat. But as these people come under Manipur, they are outside the scope of this book.

As regards cultivation, two methods are observed by these tribes—the Angāmis mostly cultivate on terraced hill sides, all other tribes by the system called "jhooming," namely, clearing strips of hill side of jungle which is burnt on the ground, the ash making a good manure. Several crops are grown on it annually, and the soil is very soon impoverished. The community then clear fresh hill sides, the former land being allowed to recuperate for some ten years by means of the jungle which soon covers it again. To a stranger suddenly arriving in the Angāmi country nothing strikes him with greater surprise and admiration than the beautiful terraced cultivation which meets the eye everywhere, on gentle hill slopes, sides and bottoms of valleys, in fact, wherever the land can be utilised in this way. In preparation, upkeep, and irrigation, the very greatest care is taken, far in excess of anything seen in the north-west Himalayas. The appearance of the countryside for miles south of Kohima, for instance, is such as to suggest the handiwork and labour of a far higher order of people than these wild Nagas. These terraced fields are often bordered with dwarf alder bushes, are carefully irrigated by an elaborate system of channels bringing water down from mountain streams, and luxuriant crops of rice are grown on them. To pass through the valley where stand the two powerful villages of Khonoma and Mozema during late October when the crops are ripe is indeed a delight for the eye—a

BURIAL TREE OUTSIDE TABHLUNG VILLAGE, WESTERN PATKOI, A CORPSE FASTENED TO TRUNK A LITTLE WAY UP, WRAPPED ROUND WITH LEAVES, SKULLS AT BASE OF TREE.

veritable golden valley. The further south and east one goes beyond this tribe the less attention is paid to this form of cultivation, though it is still found in the hills away east of Bhamo ; but in upper Burma the "jhooming" system, or "tawnya," as the Burmese call it, is far more in vogue. Amongst all these Naga tribes social customs demand that the young unmarried men sleep in a house set apart for them; while in some tribes, such as the Aohs, the unmarried girls also sleep together in a small house apart from their families. Where the young men reside is known as the "dekha chang," and in it are hung spoils of the chase, of war, and weapons. Amongst the Aohs, Semas, Langtas, and Trans-Dikkoo Nagas are seen "Morangs," not unlike those found in Borneo among the Dyāk villages, namely, large substantial timber and thatched houses of peculiar shape, one of which stands close to the entrance of the "khel," or parish one might call it, into which all Naga villages are divided up. Alongside of these "Morangs," which are of the nature of guard-houses, stands the war drum hollowed out of a huge tree trunk, and beaten in times of peril to the community to call the men back from the distant fields, or on occasions of festivity and ceremonial. The sound emitted is deep, vibrating, and travels far. All young men have to put in a certain period of duty at the "Morang," which forms a rude sort of military system, and when ended the man cuts a slab of a certain tree and sets it up in front of the guard house, in token that his tour of duty is over. Amongst these tribes heads taken and other trophies of war are hung in their "Morangs," and some of the enormous timbers supporting the roofs will be found elaborately carved with representations of elephants, lizards, toucan heads (the greater hornbill), and nude human figures. All these tribes are head-hunters, but such trophies are seldom

AOH NAGA CHIEF'S HOUSE.

seen on our side of the border nowadays; though just across the Dikkoo river (the border) this pastime is indulged in as vigorously as ever. The writer recalls having seen, when at Yāsim village on a punitive expedition in 1900, the two headmen's house fronts adorned, one with thirty-seven, the other with forty-two, human skulls attached to a sort of trellis work, each skull being embellished with a goat's horn fixed on each side. These people are usually very friendly disposed, courteous in their independent way, and willing to assist Europeans. It is only in the nearer proximity to our headquarter stations and civilisation that these pleasant qualities are found somewhat lacking. Much intercourse with Europeans seems to breed bad manners, impertinence, and refusal of aid; and it must be said that the pampering of them frequently by English officials, and the absence of adequate punishment for insolence, has only fostered these undesirable feelings. Most Naga villages—certainly amongst the Angāmis—have wealthy funds from which they pay with ease the paltry fines regarded as ample punishment by some of our officials, and which the people do not regard as anything approaching to what they know should be meted out to them on occasions. So wealthy are some of these funds that when carriers were being raised amongst the tribes for transport work in the Ābor expedition of 1911, a certain village was known to have given men of less rich villages Rs. 100 a man to those who would go as substitutes for their own unwilling men. The first time the Nagas are noticed in history is through the Ahom "buranjis," and show that as far back as 1530 the Nagas of Nāmsang and Tabhlung on the

Dikkoo river, within twelve miles of our present Military Police outpost at Tamlu, were sufficiently powerful to defeat an Ahom force and capture several guns. Mention is again made in 1648 of considerable trouble with the Nagas of Lakma, a big village lying some fifteen miles into the hills east of Charaideo, which in 1900 was visited by the Deputy Commissioner and an escort who found them anything but a warlike folk. The end of that century

TRANS DIKKOO NAGA AND HIS "HEADS."

saw more Naga raids put down drastically, and an embankment called the Naga Alli raised as a protection against their incursions. It seems that they, in common with all the different tribes, seized the opportunity of harrying the Assam plains during the chaotic conditions arising in Gaurinath's reign in the early part of the nineteenth century. But it is not till 1832 that Englishmen came into contact with them, when Captains Jenkins and Pemberton, on duty with the Manipuri durbar, crossed with a large escort into the Assam valley from that State, coming out at Nagura, and had to fight the whole

CORNER IN BEREMA VILLAGE, KACCHA NAGA.

way. This passage through their country irritated the Nagas to such an extent that British troops were sent to Mohun Dijoa, on the eastern border of our Nowgong district, to protect that part of the border which then ran along the foot of the hills. To obviate any trouble accruing to ourselves from these tribes it was proposed that the Manipur State should control all the Naga hills as far as the Doyang river and down to the North Cachar hills; and in 1835 the forest land between the Dhansiri and Doyang rivers was declared the boundary between Assam and Manipur. In the same year trouble arose through our villages in North Cachar being subjected to Naga raids and exactions, and as neither Manipur nor Tularam, who ruled in the North Cachar hills did anything to stop the outrages, and as it was found that Manipuri occupation of the hills only exasperated the tribes, Government found itself obliged to take some action. An English official, Mr. Grange, Assistant at Nowgong, was in 1838 empowered to raise a small Cachar levy—the starting-point of the present well-known Naga Hills Military Police Battalion —to preserve order and to defend the border. In the following year continued trouble led to the first British expedition into the Angāmi country, but owing to insufficiency of troops and transport, Grange only got as far as Berema and retired out of the hills, visiting Sāmāguting a large village on the outer range east of Dimāpur, where he strongly advocated the establishment of a permanent military post instead of the unhealthy one at Mohun Dijoa.

It was now determined to re-align another definite boundary between Assam and Manipur, and the watershed of the great Barail range was settled on, our side of the same being controlled from Nowgong. In 1840, to receive the Angāmi's submission and to meet and define this boundary with the Manipuri officials, Grange again entered the hills at Sāmāguting and reached Paplongmai, where he found the Manipuris had turned back without waiting for him, so he followed them on for two marches. At Togwema, finding the Nagas avowedly hostile to Manipur, and they deeming Grange to be an ally of their enemies, he was attacked by a combination of villages, of which he managed to burn five before leaving the hills. The effect of this outing apparently stopped raiding for a time, and a Lieutenant Biggs was sent into the Angāmi hills in 1841 to prospect for a suitable route to Manipur and to make friends with villages. He met with no opposition, concluded friendly agreements, and opened a salt depot at their request at Dimapur. Satisfactory arrangements over the boundary not having been yet arrived at, in 1842 Biggs marched through to Manipur, and in conference with Captain Gordon, then Political Agent at Manipur, the actual boundary was laid down in detail almost as it is to this day. But proposals for a British post at Paplongmai

A TANKHUL NAGA FROM MANIPUR.

and a road to Sāmāguting were negatived. In 1844 an Assistant from Nowgong entered the hills to collect the tribute agreed upon by them with Biggs. The chiefs, however, defied him, and practically chased him out of the country, falling at the same time on one of our outposts, which they completely destroyed. This led to Captain Eld's expedition in 1844, which exacted considerable retribution and burnt some villages, for which Eld in the end was censured, as it was believed a village was burnt which should have been spared. After this the need of occupying the hills with a military post was again discussed, but a middle course was thought best; and in the following year Captain Butler led a force through part of the country, mapping it, and conciliating the chiefs who paid him their tribute in ivory, cloth, and spears. But the moment he was out of the hills the old raiding parties started again. Butler led another expedition to the Angāmis, and the same farce of agreements and oaths was gone through; but he succeeded in starting a market at Sāmāguting, and in making a road there from Dimāpur, which had now become quite a trading centre. Butler had left behind him a police official named Bogchand at Sāmāguting with authority over the hill people. This official, while proceeding to settle disputes at Mozema, was attacked at Piphima where, disdaining precautions, his escort was dispersed and he himself was killed. To avenge this, Captain Vincent headed a force armed with powers to destroy villages and granaries of any who were hostile; it having been pointed out to Government that our punishments were too mild, and the Nagas thought far more of the Manipuris than of us. Vincent entered the hills in December, 1849, but was not successful, due to the Commandant falling ill; two villages were burnt, but the troops had to retreat, and the Nagas celebrated the occasion by serious raids on the plains. Signs of hostile stirring were manifest amongst other sections than the Angāmis.

KEKRIMA, ANGĀMI NAGA VILLAGE SHOWING THE CURIOUS HORNED ORNAMENTATION TO HOUSES OF WEALTHY MEN.

Manipur was fermenting the disturbances by intrigue, and strong repressive measures were eminently required. In 1850 Vincent therefore led a stronger force over the border, and succeeded in penetrating to the two chief offending villages of Khonoma and Mozema, which were attacked and burnt. He then established himself in a strong stockade commanding this part of the tribal country, from which he made tours and punished several other sections during the summer. Next winter another column under Captain Blake with two guns was sent up to assist Vincent, when a Naga fort was captured near Khonoma, and the two officers with a strong force visited Kohima and part of the eastern Angāmi country, being opposed at Kekrima village, where the Angāmis fought well in the open, and Vincent only won after what the official reports styled "a bloody battle."

Many arguments now took place over two lines of policy, namely, retaining military hold of the hills, or abandoning them entirely; the latter course, from economical considerations, being finally adopted, all troops were withdrawn entirely from the hills and their immediate vicinity, the Nowgong border being protected by a line of outposts from Golaghat, namely, Borpathar, Mohun Dijoa, Asāloo, Gūnjong, and the tribes were left to riot at their own sweet will. It is amusing and interesting to note the immediate and natural results of this policy. Reports of those days show the jubilant Nagas when once they realised they were left alone, celebrated the new conditions by making twenty-two serious raids that year into British territory, *i.e.*, down into the main Assam valley where the tea industry was progressing. This alone showed the impracticability of non-interference; yet in spite of the urgent protests of the frontier officials, and requests to be allowed to make reprisals, the game went on until 1862, when the Commissioner represented to Government the intolerable state of affairs. It was four more years before this simple matter was definitely taken up, and Government then directed a strong outpost to be located at Sāmāguting, on the outer fringe of the hills, where Lieutenant Gregory was sent as Deputy Commissioner, armed with powers of punishment. This produced a good effect for a time, and about

ANGĀMI NAGA GRAVE—MAN'S

1874, as all seemed quiet, survey operations were extended into the hills with disturbing effect. Two parties entered, the northern one under Captain Badgeley and Lieutenant Holcombe with a strong escort from Sibsagor ; the southern one under Captain Butler from Sāmāguting into the Lhota Naga country. Both parties were attacked, the northern one in 1874 coming utterly to grief at Ninu, three marches into the hills, when the Nagas attacked the camp treacherously and made a huge bag (as is related elsewhere), namely, Holcombe and eighty men killed, Badgeley and fifty wounded ; while later, in 1875, Butler's party walked into an ambuscade at Pangti village, he losing his life and his men being dispersed. A punitive column under Colonel Nuthall with some of the 44th Sylhet Light Infantry and of the 42nd Native Infantry were sent into the hills, stayed a short while, met no opposition, and, having exacted an incomplete amount of retribution, returned to the plains.

Gregory at Sāmāguting meanwhile had had to punish neighbouring villages at different times, and both he and Butler in the early days of the new outposts were able to make several satisfactory visits to large villages in the hills. But after the disasters to the survey parties, the Chief Commissioner urged a forward policy most strongly, and the establishment of a post well into the hills from which to dominate these turbulent people, as the present state of affairs, he said, was most discreditable to our rule. Before any decision could be arrived at by Government, the large village of Mozema started raiding, and a force of 230 sepoys under Captain Brydon, with Mr. Carnegie as Political Officer, advanced from Sāmāguting, and in December, 1877, attacked and burnt Mozema. The defenders dispersing and joined by the villages of Jotsoma and Khonoma, harried

Sāmāguting and the line of communication; and a hundred sepoys of the 43rd Assam Light Infantry were sent up to reinforce Brydon. The end of these operations can only be described as ridiculous, for the Political Officer Mr. Williamson, who succeeded Mr. Carnegie, on the latter being killed accidentally by one of our sentries, let off Khonoma and Jotsoma scot free, while he merely imposed on Mozema a

ANGĀMI NAGA GRAVE—WOMAN'S. HER BASKETS, WEAVING STICKS, AND DOMESTIC UTENSILS.

fine of Rs. 50 and made them give up four of their guns, and what they had looted from three constables and a mail bag. These absurdly lenient terms having been complied with, the force returned to Sāmāguting. The Chief Commissioner's forward policy was now approved of, and Kohima being decided on as a suitable situation to control the Angāmis from, and Wokha for the same purpose in the Lhota Naga country further north, in 1878 troops were sent up, and stockaded posts built at both places, Mr. Damant being detailed as Deputy Commissioner of the Naga hills. For a year all went well, till in May, 1879, Damant found that the large village of Khonoma was collecting arms and ammunition, and before long this section showed decided hostility. The fact being the people now realised the existence of this garrison (200 rifles) effectively stopped their head hunting

KOHIMA VILLAGE—ANGĀMI NAGA—900 HOUSES.

and raiding pursuits, entailed payment of tribute, the supply of men as transport carriers; and all this they resented. In spite of evidences of unrest, such as an abortive attack on the post at Piphima, Damant did not believe it was likely to be serious, and before starting out for a tour in the north he visited Khonoma (twelve miles off) to find out the temper of the people. In October, 1879, with an escort of twenty-five Regulars and sixty-five Military Police, he passed through Jotsoma and reached the foot of the hill on which stands Khonoma. Leaving his baggage at a little stream below, he ascended the narrow path with only one or two sepoys, the rest of the escort coming on leisurely. On arrival at the village gate he found it closed, and his demands for admittance were answered by a volley which killed Damant and the Sepoys with him, and the next moment the escort was attacked, beaten back down the narrow path, and almost annihilated at the stream where the baggage was looted. Fifty-seven in all were killed and wounded, and the remainder got back to Kohima as best they could. This station, in which were Mr. Cawley of the Police, with Mrs. Cawley and Mrs. Damant and 180 rifles, was at once besieged, and a few days later received a small reinforcement of twenty-two rifles under Mr. Hinde from Wokha, and were only relieved a fortnight later by Colonel Johnstone, Political Agent at Imphal, with 2,000 Manipuri soldiers and forty sepoys of the 34th N.I. The Kohima garrison had an uncommonly unpleasant experience, being surrounded by some six to seven thousand Naga warriors, who spared no effort to fire the thatched buildings and attacked the stockade repeatedly by rolling heavy timbers forward along the ground behind which they sheltered and fired.

General Nation was now directed to assemble a force of 1,135 men with two mountain guns at Golaghat, and in early November these moved forward and entered the hills, not without considerable opposition at the villages of Sephema and Sachima. From the latter place as a base four miles from the objective, Nation attacked Khonoma on the 22nd November, 1879. It was by nature very strong, and had been rendered far more so by the Nagas with infinite labour and skill; and standing as it does on a steep spur jutting out into the valley, it formed a difficult nut to crack, the surrounding hills being too far off and too difficult to permit of good turning

CARVED FRONT TO A WEALTHY NAGA'S HOUSE.

movements. The assault lasted all day and slowly the troops forced their way up through the lower village defences until the upper ones were reached, but not till nightfall. Many hand-to-hand conflicts occurred, and many were killed and wounded, and it was decided to stay the night on the ground won and assault the upper works at dawn. This was done, but the works were found deserted, the Nagas having withdrawn in the night to the Chakka Fort far up in the Barail range overlooking the village. Our losses in this affair were two British officers and the Subahdar Major of the 44th S.L.I. killed, two British and two Native officers wounded, and forty-four sepoys killed and wounded. Khonoma was strongly garrisoned, and the rest of the force visited and punished various other villages; while for months the Khonoma men held the Chakka position and carried on a guerilla war, even raiding as far as the Bālādhan tea garden, eighty-eight miles off in Cachar. The supplies also of the Khonoma and Paplongmai posts were frequently interrupted and looted, so a strict blockade of the Chakka Forts being made and reinforcements reaching both posts, the Nagas finally gave in and submitted on the 28th of March, 1880. It is also conceivable that the drastic punishment meted out by Colonel Johnstone on Phesema village who attacked his convoys during the winter may have somewhat taken the heart out of the Angāmis, who were in the end well punished by fines in cash and grain, unpaid labour, the surrender of firearms, and demolition of defences; while Khonoma in addition had all its cultivated lands confiscated, and its inhabitants dispersed among other clans.

Since then this powerful tribe have remained quiet, though in 1891, at the time of the Manipur rebellion, it was found that the rebel durbar of that State was intriguing with Khonoma, so a Sikh regiment (the 36th) was brought to Golaghat, whose presence near their hills was instrumental in keeping the Khonoma people quiet. It may here be remarked that after a few years Government permitted the resumption of their old village site by this section of the Angāmis. This marked the end of serious trouble and hostility in the Naga hills, but it was found desirable during succeeding years to extend our rule northwards to the Aoh and Lengta Naga country to still further put

STOCKADED ENTRANCE TO MONGSIN VILLAGE, TRANS DIKKOO.

an end to petty raids in the plains, and in 1890 the Naga hills revenue paying district extended from the Henema outpost in the south close to the North Cachar hills to the Tamlu post in the north at the corner where the Dikkoo river turns to emerge into the plains, a length of some 250 miles. This latter river has up to now been our border line here, which further south becomes the line of the Tizoo and

Lanier rivers, east of which the country is "unadministered," the wild tribes being left to themselves as long as they do not worry our side of the border. This, however, they have done now and again, notably in 1888, when the big village of Mongsemdi was badly raided by the men of the Trans-Dikkoo

SEMA CHIEF'S HOUSE. CARVED TREE TRUNKS DENOTE WEALTH.

villages of Litam and Noksen, which called forth a punitive expedition and both villages were burnt with some opposition. It has frequently occurred that the Trans-Dikkoo villages more adjacent to our border have begged to be taken over by us, when the condition of "alarums and excursions" to which they are subjected by their savage neighbours would be ended. This further extension of the border up to the present has naturally not found favour in the eyes of Government. As showing the condition of preparedness against attack in which these people constantly dwell, the writer was across the border at Bor Tabhlung in 1899 with a Civil Officer and a small escort to inquire into some land dispute, when the women of the village were seen going out in the morning to work in their fields armed like their men with heavy "daos." This, in order to be able to protect themselves against surprise attack by another village which had started raiding. A state of insecurity for the people, which must become intolerable at times, although they have ever been accustomed to it.

All the outposts are now connected with the headquarter station at Kohima by good, well-graded bridle paths which are now extended in several directions into the Sema hills with comfortable rest-houses at all stages. A broad metalled cart road also connects Dimapur on the railway with Kohima, forty-seven miles, continuing on through the hills eighty-eight miles further to Manipur.

CHAPTER XV

REGRETTABLE INCIDENTS, TREACHERY, METHODS OF FIGHTING, ETC.

It may not be generally known that the various disasters and regrettable incidents that have from time to time occurred in the past on this north-eastern border have all been due to neglect of proper precautions, half-hearted measures, and unpreparedness. Prominent examples of this are to be found in White's disaster at Sadiya in 1839, Lowther's in 1858, Holcombe's at Ninu in 1874, Butler's at Pangti the following year, Damant's at Khonoma in 1879, Manipur in 1891, and others. Of these it may be as well to give in detail the story of Holcombe's affair, while the incident in Shimong village towards the end of the recent Ābor expedition, although no blood was shed, proved the Ābors' intention, and goes to show what the treachery of these tribes is like and which, ever to be guarded against, was in both these cases neglected. Holcombe and Badgeley, with a strong military escort and train of coolies, had gone some three marches into the hills (east of Sibsagor) for survey work, and had camped in the vicinity of Ninu village. The next morning early a large party of Nagas, apparently friendly, entered the camp and approached Holcombe, who was strolling about. The sepoys were all cooking their food, only one sentry was posted over the front of the camp, and Captain Badgeley was still dressing in his tent. Through an interpreter Holcombe chatted with the head man of the party, one of whom asked to be shown a rifle. The nearest one happened to be that in the sentry's hand, which Holcombe took and showed. This was the signal, for the next moment the savages threw off their blankets, under which each had his "dao," Holcombe and the sentry were cut down dead at once, and the enemy rushed through the camp, cutting down sepoys before they could get to their weapons, and everyone within reach. Badgeley was cut at and wounded as he left his tent, but succeeded in collecting a few sepoys and making a stand while rifles were got out. The stand, however, was of short duration, and a retreat had to be made fortunately well conducted, or none would have returned at all. The affair was over in a very short time and the camp and its vicinity swarming with the exultant enemy, who had accounted for Holcombe and eighty men killed, Badgeley and fifty wounded, and were now busy making their bag of heads. Badgeley with his small party effected a retirement out of the hills with such of the wounded as they could take.

When the Ābor expedition, 1911–12, was drawing to its close and an exploration and survey outing was in progress, a party of some one hundred rifles and six British officers reached the neighbourhood of Shimong and camped below, sending word up to the village of their presence and calling on the

Gām (head man) to come in. This was met by a refusal either to come in or to allow the party to pass up further. Next morning the Civil Officer in charge with all the British officers and ten rifles only, started ahead, leaving the remaining rifles to come on with the Naga carriers. They entered the village, and in the large sort of open market-place in the centre found a gathering of some three to four hundred armed Ābors who at once drew their "daos." The Civil officer, waving a handkerchief, called to them that we had no hostile intention, whereupon they put up their weapons, broke up, and began to mingle with our people, the sepoys, who had moved forward on seeing the hostile attitude, having been ordered back behind the British officers. Through the interpreter our officers talked with the Gām, the while his warriors began pushing in between our people ostensibly to examine their clothes, equipment, etc., till the little party were all separated, some being so handled by Ābors as to have buttons and shoulder straps pulled off, while one sepoy had his rifle snatched away, which, however, he regained next moment. When the Gām in reply to an officer's remark that they were now going on, said, "No, you are not," and following it up by adding, "and you are not going back either," things were realised to be exceedingly serious. Fortunately, all kept their heads, and the parley continued, the while every member of the party was firmly held —in many cases with their arms behind their backs —by three or four Ābors. Presently the head of the column, a Native officer with some twenty-five rifles appeared at the far end of the village, and the officers asking to be allowed to sit in the shade of a big tree in the open space, the tribesmen released them, and the party moved to the tree, the ten rifles immediately taking post in front of the Ābor gathering at the same moment as the Native officer's party swung into the market-place, who, grasping the situation, at once moved his men to the other side of the hostile crowd. These, now between two fires had they attempted any rush, began to laugh and treat the episode as one of humour and joke, which it most certainly was not. Had the Ābors only made up their minds at once all would have been over with the entire party, for not one could have done anything in self-defence. As it was, they delayed just too long and their opportunity passed. The little force returned to its camp below that night, and next morning, well closed up and with bayonets fixed, they passed through Shimong village, which now held only about one hundred Ābors, and pursued their route up the Dihang. Not long after a post of fifty rifles was established here from Kebang as one of the supply depots to Bentinck's party exploring up the Dihang. Another account says the force did not pass through this village again, but proceeded on by another route. This very dangerous episode came about by approaching a village of hostile intentions in a happy-go-lucky way more

"JEKIA," A SEMA NAGA CHIEF.

worthy of schoolboys than men, and also was due in a measure to the strict adherence to orders not to fire unless in self-defence, and generally, in fact, to subordinate all dignity of procedure to the present-day absurd sentiment of " making friends " or " back-patting," and this in a hostile country!

Butler and Damant both came to grief, in the Lhota and Angāmi country respectively, by approaching villages of doubtful temper with no ordinary military precautions. It is generally said that none of these tribes ever fight in the open or have any heart for aught save night surprises and village defences, or wherever treachery points the way to success. This is certainly generally true, but it must not be forgotten that instances have occurred of fighting in the open. Captain Charlton's operations in 1845 against the Singphos included an open daylight fight near Bisa; while in 1851, near Kekrima village in the eastern Angāmi country, Captains Vincent and Blake were resolutely attacked on a rolling open plateau below and about a mile from the village defences, the Angāmis making a great effort against Blake's two guns and only drawing off with great loss, while ours was by no means inconsiderable.

The late General Macgregor, who had extensive experiences amongst these various tribes, used to speak well of their bravery on occasions, particularly of the Angāmi Nagas, and cited several instances when he had seen them come out into the open under our fire and carry off their wounded.

In February, 1900, the Deputy Commissioner of the Naga Hills and the Commandant with one hundred rifles of the Kohima Military Police Battalion, were *en route* to the Sibsagor Hinterland to exact punishment for a series of petty raids, and while crossing a strip of "unadministered country" were seriously attacked by the inhabitants of a large and hitherto unvisited village of Yachumi. Here the tribesmen

SEMA WARRIOR WEARING THEIR CURIOUS TAIL ORNAMENT.

attacked the column on the side of a hill a little distance from their village about noon, coming on in a large mob of armed men after they had executed a war dance, which was seen through glasses by the Deputy Commissioner and the Commandant. Only as a last resource and to keep them from getting near enough to create a panic among the coolies, did fire open; and it was then seen that these people had no idea whatever of firearms, the first rounds going over did not attract their attention; the next hit two men, and struck up the ground in front of the mob, who at once stopped to look at the wounded, while others began digging in the ground with spear butts to see what was being thrown at them with so much noise. It did not stop the rush, however, which came nearer, until nineteen or twenty were down close in front of the advance guard. This checked them, and as our flankers on the slopes above called down that the Nagas were gathering in strength in the forest above to attack the flank of the long, winding column, the Commandant, taking a section of twenty-five rifles, climbed the hill and cleared the gathering away. The enemy retreated into their village and stoutly opposed our entrance, losing many more in so doing. They used spears and daos and a heavy cross-bow with short poisoned arrows which carried over 150 yards. This village, a large one of 500 houses or more, was then burnt and the little column proceeded on its way north by another route, as too much hostility was anticipated from other large villages seen in the neighbourhood. This people attacked in the open, and did not give way until some forty-five of them were killed, while on our side three men were badly wounded by spears and several more by "pānjis."

The attack of Trans-Dikkoo Nagas of the Chinlong and Chinkoi villages, just across the Dikkoo river from Tamlu, on a Military Police column of some 200 rifles in February, 1913, who were *en route* to punish the tribe for raiding for heads on our side of the border, took place in the day time and on fairly open hills and spurs. Being absolutely surprised, although warning had been given that these people did mean to fight which was generally disbelieved, the column lost several sepoys and many transport coolies both shot and cut down; and at one time, as panic set in amongst the coolies, things looked for a bit extremely awkward. Of the losses to the Nagas little or nothing was known, but they drew off towards evening. A stronger force was shortly afterwards sent up which, having a practically free hand, went through those hills and exacted possibly the most complete amount of reparation of any previous expedition since the "'fifties," and did it in a remarkably short time. The operations of this column have now led to the placing of a military post in the Tantok hills to preserve order, the border line having been advanced eastwards some distance.

From these and other instances of fighting in the open it is apparent that the original tactics of these tribes have been modified to suit the situation of contending with an enemy generally better armed and, in these days, with modern rifles, when attacks *en masse* can only have a disastrous ending to those making them. Surely then, they can with greater justice be called astute rather than altogether cowardly. Their tactics are the best that can be devised to suit their numbers, weapons, and country, so we can hardly blame these savages for not more often meeting us out in the open. For instance, in the Chin hills, whose people and country are not very dissimilar to those we have discussed, Mr. Carey, in his account of the subjugation of this tribe, describes how when he first met them they fought in the open, but soon found they and their flintlocks were no match for our sepoys and rifles. They then changed their tactics and fought from covered-in trenches as at Tartan in 1889. The following year it was found that they had again changed their methods in hope of withstanding our troops, and the lines of guerilla warfare were followed—harrying convoys, cutting up small parties, planning ambuscades, firing into camps at night, and so forth.

CHAPTER XVI

THE NORTH-EASTERN FRONTIER GENERALLY AND ITS MILITARY POLICE FORCES

HAVING traced the history of this long stretch of borderland from old times, the reasons which brought the English up to it, and the tribes dwelling along the same, we can turn to the present outlook of affairs and see what future possibilities may hold for us. We have seen that the last big expedition against the Ābors had a greater importance and interest owing to what is spoken of as the awakening of China and the modernising of her forces. The new condition began to call for notice by the European nations brought into touch with her about 1908, the matter concerning us at first over Chinese action in Thibet —a country whose unknown south-eastern districts are in touch somewhere with the Ābor and Mishmi tribe. Our having given over Thibet practically to Chinese rule after the Thibet expedition of 1904–05 resulted a few years later in the latter's troops overrunning the country, garrisons being established at Phari and in the Chumbi valley, contiguous to the Sikkim border, which is directly under British control. The Chumbi valley had been held by our troops until Thibet had paid the war indemnity, when they were withdrawn to India. Chinese rule in Thibet during 1911 became weakened by risings of the people of the country, and more troops were sent in there from Ssü-chuan to restore order but failed, largely owing to considerable difficulties due to the opposition of tribesmen in south-eastern Thibet, where in several actions the Chinese were barely able to hold their own, and such reinforcements as could be spared were sent down the Tsan-Po from Thibet; such action more or less coinciding with the opening of the Ābor expedition of 1911–12. About the same time reports came to hand that the Chinese who had occupied Rima east of the Mishmi hills were sending emissaries amongst that tribe to secure their submission. Various aggressive acts of the Chinese at points along the Burma border then occurred, notably west of the Salween-Irrawadi divide in 1910–11, when a Military Police Force was sent to the Hpimaw group of villages for their protection. Our frontier outpost line was then extended to Htawgaw, some sixty miles from Myitkhyina and east of the Nmai-kha on the Ngawchang river. Later Chinese activity in this direction tending to disturb the equanimity of the tribes led to a Military Police outpost being located at Hpimaw itself in 1913, and the frontier road extended up to it. A few miles east of Hpimaw two easy passes cross the range overlooking the Salween river and form a small trade route into the Tengyueh Province of China. The new Hpimaw post stands at an elevation of 8,500 feet and will be held by one hundred rifles under two British officers. It lies sixteen marches from Myitkhyina among the tribes of Lashis and Yawyins, of whom the latter only are held in considerable estimation by our officers, who are disposed to have them tried as fighting material formed into a sort of frontier militia. It is known the Chinese utilise numbers of Yawyins in their Yünnanese forces.

In fact it would seem that China had been desirous of extending her rule right up to our borders, and that this was possibly a fixed principle of her statesmen in the past. It may so happen that under a new and stable government and a rapidly modernising China this idea will come to the front again. Hence much interest has been shifted from the north-west to the north-east borders of India, and efforts are being made to lift the veil hitherto covering this vast tract of country, as we have seen, by various exploring and survey parties. The success of their efforts from Assam has been mentioned, and similarly those from Myitkhyina in Upper Burma have increased our knowledge of the unknown lands between the Mali-kha and Nmai-kha rivers and the important watersheds between the Irrawadi and Salween rivers, while the parties which entered the little-known region of Hkāmti Lông have effected much in exploration and survey. Thus on the Burma borderland we now see the results of the survey operations, 1911–12–13, in an accurate survey of the Salween-Irrawadi watershed up to latitude 28° 20′, which nearly joins up with the work of M. Bacot and Captain Bailey in 1911 at the sources of the Irrawadi. In fact, there is now only a gap of some 10°, so that for all practical purposes this watershed can be fixed on the map as far north as latitude 28° 45′, where lie the northernmost sources of that river. The course of the N'mai-kha, the most easterly and hitherto unknown tributary of the Irrawadi, has also been traced and mapped throughout, and its main tributaries, the Tarôn and Nām Tamai, have been surveyed up to latitudes 28° 20′ and 28° 15′ respectively. Our knowledge of the great Irrawadi basin is thus practically complete.

The efforts of Captains Pritchard and Waterfield were most successful along the Nām Tamai river (or Adungwang as it is called in its upper reaches) up to the village of Lama-nay, which was found to be the furthest inhabited spot; while their journey up the Tarôn, the easterly tributary of the N'mai-kha, extended as far as latitude 28° 20′, where they were then within only a few days' march of the Mekhong-Rima route which was traversed by Captain Bailey in 1911. The lamented death of Captain Pritchard, who was drowned in the Tarōn river in the late spring of 1913, put a stop to the further efforts of this party, and lost to us an intrepid explorer and one whose work in the recent past has been invaluable. Behind these parties road-making has been pushed on as far as possible towards the border land, a good bridle path having been completed and telegraph communication established between the garrison of Myitkhyina and the outposts of Htawgaw and Hpimaw. Other remotely possible contingencies connected with Thibet and the more distant parts of this borderland no doubt exist, but their very remoteness renders it undesirable to allude to them at present.

Large schemes for defence have hitherto only concerned the other side of India, defence against internal trouble alone being arranged for in Assam. This country has no main roads bridged or metalled throughout, while the chief means of transport are the Brahmaputra steamers and the Assam-Bengal Railway, the latter being of but limited capacity. In view of the unexpected always occurring, and trouble coming from without, to be most likely accompanied by trouble from within, a grave situation might arise in regard to these rich provinces of Assam and Upper Burma.

The interest into which this borderland has sprung may, it is hoped, favourably affect the matter of communications in both provinces, as the present condition of most roads would prove a very considerable difficulty in moving large bodies of troops in the event of prolonged and extensive military operations in either Assam or Upper Burma.

Many people argue that there is no danger to this side of India owing to its difficulties in the way of mountains, forests, and rivers; but they are probably unaware of the fact that China carried out only a little over one hundred years ago what has been spoken of as "the most remarkable military achievement known," namely, when she moved an army of 70,000 men over 2,000 miles of most difficult mountainous country at great altitudes through Thibet into Nepal, defeating the Goorkhas at Tengri Maidan and crushing them at their capital. What they effected then in setting all these impediments at naught, it is not unreasonable to suppose could be done again.

The Burmese also, as we have seen, invaded and took Assam early in the last century, the forests and difficulties of the Patkoi mountains proving not insurmountable to them. Huge stones set up and carved with the peacock—the royal bird of Burma—denoting the halting-place of some general and his troops, have been found in the heart of the Naga hills, showing that they did not all move by the more easy passes of the northern Patkoi. Against the establishment of military posts among these tribes it is frequently argued that it means taking over the whole area and thereby adding to the burden of administration; but this need not be the case. It was not so in the Singpho country, where such posts were held for a few years and withdrawn when the tribe was settled and recognised our power. We have not been into their country since, nor have they given us further trouble. The establishment of military posts was found to be the only way of impressing the Nagas with ideas of law and order; in this case, however, it was found desirable to take over and administer the country, but it does not follow in all cases that this would necessarily be carried out.

These posts among savage tribes are the only means of really controlling them, and must prove cheapest in the end, when we see the great expense occurring and recurring of punitive expeditions entering only the outer fringe of the hills and coming out again, often without exacting what the tribes recognise as punishment, and which system they are too prone to look on as a sign of weakness.

The Military Police Force.

The early years after the annexation of Upper Burma being times of much trouble and the employment of large numbers of regular troops, brought about the establishment of Military Police Battalions, to augment the Civil Police and also to assist the Regular troops. These latter ceased to be on a field force footing about April, 1888, and were reduced ; and at the same time the Military Police Force stood at a strength of 13,300, which a year or so later was increased to 18,000 men.

They are a force entirely under the Civil Government, dressed, drilled, and trained as regulars, but for political reasons in the matter of arms they are kept, as one might say, a pace behind, *i.e.*, where the latter are armed with the latest patterns of rifles, the Military Police Battalions have Martinis. To work this large machine officers are lent from the army to the Civil Government as Commandants and Assistant Commandants for a term of two to five years to train and discipline these battalions, while numbers of Native officers and men are transferred from the Indian Army to assist in the same purpose. The particular corps which keep watch and ward over the Upper Burma borderland are the Chindwyn Military Police Battalion with headquarters at Monywa, and detachments far up that river almost to the Hukong valley ; the Myitkhyina Military Police Battalion with headquarters at that station on the Irrawadi river in the extreme north of Burma, with strong detachments at Sadōn and Simā facing that part of the China border, and which has lately located outposts some distance up the Nmai-kha river ; the Bhamo Military Police Battalion with outposts far up the Taping and Shweli rivers ; the Northern Shan States Military Police Battalion with headquarters at Lashio and outposts stretching along the northern border from the Shweli to the Salween rivers. These outposts of each battalion are more or less closely linked with each other, while the Chindwyn Military Police Battalion with its western outpost at Tammoo links up the chain with the outposts of the Manipur State, and these again further north with the Military Police Battalion of the Naga hills in Assam. So that for purposes of resisting tribal aggression the chain is fairly complete. Further east and south our outposts of the southern Shan States Military Police Battalion, which locality does not however come within the scope of this work, face those of the French at no great distance in the Trans-Salween country and Mekhong valley.

These Military Police Battalions have had changes in organisation since their starting-point in 1886. For instance, for many years there were two Chindwyn Battalions—the upper at Kendat, the lower at Monywa; while the old Mogoung Levy, which did such good hard service under Captain (now General) O'Donnell in the early days of constant raid and trouble, ceased to exist as Military Police on the establishment of the Myitkhyina Military Police Battalion, when Mogoung, at one time the headquarters, dwindled down to an outpost. Peaceful conditions all up the Chindwyn similarly did not require two strong corps, and now one is sufficient for duty in that locality. These frontier Military Police Battalions mostly enlist men from Northern India, but have also two or three companies of Goorkhas recruited from eastern Nepal, while the Myitkhyina Military Police Battalion is entirely composed of this latter class, and the Bhamo Military Police Battalion has two companies of Kachins who are spoken of very favourably as soldiers. In Burma most of the Military Police Battalions have two or three companies of Mounted Infantry belonging to them, and these owing to the large number of cavalry officers who take service in this force are very carefully attended to and trained. In 1890 a number of old Madras regiments were disbanded, and in their place arose the first three Burma Regiments formed from Military Police Battalions, of which one was the old Mogoung Levy, and at the same time the strength of the force was reduced to 12,000 men, which again in later years it has been found necessary to increase.

In Assam a Military Police Force has been organised since about 1830, first as an armed Civil Force known as the Cachar Levy, and then as a Frontier Police Force. This force, as Assam was opened up and came entirely under our rule, was distributed in posts along the foot of the hills from Cooch Behar to Sadiya, thence, crossing the Brahmaputra, the posts ran along the foot of the Naga hills up the Dhansiri valley, through the North Cachar hills into Silchar, where they linked up again with the posts guarding the Lushai border. Up to 1880, although their duties were practically entirely military they were styled constables and were officered by Civil Police officials and inspectors. There were in those days as a reserve to the Frontier Police four Regular regiments stationed in Assam, the headquarters of two of them being at Shillong, of another at Dibrughar, and of a fourth at Silchar. These again had detachments about the country, the principal ones being at Gauhati, Tezpur, Golaghat, Jaipur, Sadiya in Upper Assam; and at Monierkhal, Alinagar, and Chargola in Silchar (Cachar).

Some of these were right on the border, and on the re-organisation of Assam's internal defence in 1880–81 the Frontier Police were increased and given entire charge of the border posts, the Regulars being reduced to three regiments, namely, the old 42nd, 43rd and 44th Assam Light Infantry. Two years later, for the improvement of the Frontier Police in their military duties, discipline, etc., it was found desirable to break the old force up and reconstitute it into

Usual Form of Our Stockades on N.E. Frontier.

battalions of Military Police and to borrow officers of the Regular Army as commandants to train them for a period of five years, while uniform, equipment, etc., were attended to, and the old "Brown Besses" discarded for Sniders. The force was thus organised into three full strength battalions, namely, the Lakhimpur Military Police Battalion with headquarters at Dibrughar; the Naga Hills Military Police Battalion with headquarters at Kohima; the Lushai

Military Police Battalion with headquarters at Aijal; and two battalions of lesser strength in the Garo hills at Tura, and in Cachar at Silchar. These battalions, at first of mixed enlistments, now take as many Goorkhas and Jaruas (the fighting class of Assam) as they can, the latter being good soldiers, excelling in woodcraft, rafting, building, etc.; and are, like the Goorkhas, not bothered with over much religion or caste prejudice. For many years the Lushai Military Police Battalion was the only corps in Assam which had more than one British officer—the commandant; this being due to a mutiny which occurred at Aijal about 1891 when, to bring the men into order again, two other British officers were sent as Assistant Commandants, and the retention of one of these was "managed," to obviate fear of another mutiny. The transfer to this battalion of Lungleh in the south Lushai country with its Military Police companies who hitherto had belonged to Bengal, also necessitated an additional British officer being added to the now increased battalion strength. It can thus be seen that Commandants of the other corps had their work cut out for them in order to keep their units up to a respectable condition of efficiency. And so much good work did these Commandants alone put in (with the aid of first-class Native officers, of course) that for very many years now the Assam Military Police Battalions have been perfectly fitted to stand alongside of their Regular brethren, and when employed on frontier "shows" with them have invariably earned hearty praise for their attention to duty, hard work, and discipline. People are only too prone to belittle this force generally, and to speak of them rather contemptuously as "Police," whereas they are only that in name, to distinguish the armed and disciplined forces of the Civil Government from those of the Regular army. Their duties are of an arduous nature and are purely military. That C.O.'s of regiments formerly looked askance at one of their officers going to or returning from Military Police employ is not due to the corps or the service, but simply to the bad name induced by numbers of British officers taking service with Military Police Battalions for the sole purposes of relieving the strain on their pockets and of having a slack time as they imagined, and as, of course, in their isolated positions they could have. Of course "hard bargains" of this sort did not improve during their few years in Military Police employ (if they were kept as long) and were a serious crux to their C.O.'s on return to their regiments and a proper energetic form of life. This undesirable state of affairs has now more or less ceased to exist. Commandants and Assistant Commandants who have been added to all battalions in the last eight years are carefully selected. Where in the neighbourhood of Regulars, in Assam at least, Military Police units are allowed to join in military work such as camps of exercise, etc., and Brigadiers are invited to inspect Military Police headquarters and outposts whenever they find themselves in their vicinity, which was invariably done, and it is to be hoped is kept up still. This particular method of attaining to and keeping up a reasonable degree of military efficiency does not hold in the Burma Military Police force, where pride in being "Irregulars" and a dislike to approaching anything like military rule, has led to a very distinct gulf being fixed between the two forces, and neither mix in any way even at assaults-at-arms. The Assam Military Police Battalions are also "Irregulars," but do not avoid methods of efficiency by which Commandants and Assistant Commandants know that they and their men may now and then come under the eye of the Military Head, although they are for the time being in Civil employ. It seems a pity that so little notice is ever taken of the good work which numbers of Army officers put in with the Military Police Forces, which Forces would gain considerably in efficiency if the British officers were as regularly reported on as they are in their regiments, and if at the end of their tour of service it was ordered that notes should be entered in their regimental confidential reports as to good work done or the reverse. The knowledge of this might stimulate honest workers and deter the class alluded to as "hard bargains" from either going into Military Police employ to the detriment of the same, or from staying in it any time. The writer has recently heard a useful suggestion regarding increased efficiency of this force, namely, whether it would not be advisable to institute a post of Inspecting Officer for the entire mass of Military Police Battalions, whose duties would be constant touring amongst the units, seeing their work, efficiency, and reporting at once on what was good, bad, or indifferent; with a view to the last two items being remedied at once. This particular officer to be independent of local Governments, and to deal direct with the Government of India. As things stand at present, regimental C.O.'s are usually unaware of any good work done by their officers when attached to Military Police units. The only thing they are made unpleasantly aware of is when an officer is glaringly unsatisfactory and is ordered back to his regiment—which is too rarely done. Military Police Battalions are essentially the eye and not the hand of the executive, which work falls to Regular troops on serious matter arising. But in the past, as of late years, punitive columns entirely of Military Police have been utilised and have done hard and good work which sometimes has included a small action, which (they not being Regulars) is never announced in the public papers, so they go without the benefits which accrue from advertisement. Military Police Battalions are accustomed to life and work on these borders, they can start out at a moment's notice at the wish or order of the Deputy Commissioner of the District only in time of need, coolies are impressed at once, rations weighed out, ammunition issued, the hospital assistant gets his medical pannier out, and off they go. Should a brush with a tribe occur and a casualty or two happen it is taken in the ordinary course of events and not made the subject of worry or advertisement, as is invariably the case where Regular troops are used. Hence it is obvious that to bring this very useful mobile force under the hard red-tapism of military *régime* would in no way prove to its benefit, which apparently is what is feared would occur in Burma if the two forces had anything to do with each other, except, of course, on actual service.

An interesting comparison can here be made touching the matter of expense of these Regular and Military Police expeditions. In 1889–90 an expedition (Regulars) of 1,200 troops went into the Mishmi country, to which allusion has been made earlier in these pages. The troops were out about four months, but only 120 penetrated into the main valley, and the results of the operations were disappointing; there was no active opposition at all, and the expedition cost two and a half lakhs. At the same time a small punitive outing was in progress in the hills on the south side of the Brahmaputra towards the Patkoi range, with which the late Mr. Noel Williamson went. Its strength was three British officers, two Native officers, one hundred rifles (Military Police) with 170 coolies. This little force was absent from headquarters two months, three weeks of which were spent beyond the border in most difficult and unmapped country, and where opposition was actually met with on one occasion. Its work was completed and the extra cost involved in this punitive outing was Rs. 1,766 only—truly a remarkable contrast in costliness. That Military Police life then is good for officers, or should be, goes without saying. They are paid liberally and draw travelling allowances when on duty out of their stations, while they learn what it is to be independent, what initiative and responsibility really mean, how to deal with men, and to what extent hard work can be laid upon them. Life in regiments does not teach young officers this, at least but rarely, and mostly only when they are nearing the top of the regimental tree.

APPENDIX

ROUTES.

THE chief routes towards the actual north-eastern frontier from Assam are those leading up the Dihang and Dibong rivers into Thibet now being explored, and that up the Lohit from Sadiya to Wālong, some thirty odd miles from Rima, and along which latter it is thought eventually to have a cart road.

Further through the Hkāmti Lông country, or rather into it, the only known routes towards China are those used in 1885 by Colonels Woodthorpe and Macgregor from Sadiya viâ the Nonyong Lake and a low pass of 3,960 feet in the Patkoi range up the Loglai valley past Turong Ku, who, crossing the upper Dihing, reached Hkāmti through Kumki and the Chaukan Pass; while Macgregor on another occasion explored a route across the Patkoi into the Hukong valley, and then turning north viâ Ntupntsa reached Hkāmti. This is recorded as particularly difficult.

The best line of communication between Hkāmti Lông and China is said by the inhabitants to run east to the Mali-kha river, thence down the right bank to a place spoken of as Marai Salar, whence the valley is crossed, and the path continues over ranges to the Nmai-kha and so into Yünnan.

In 1892 Mr. Errol Gray, also starting from Sadiya, explored an easier route up the Dihing valley to Kumki over the Chaukan Pass and up to the Phangma river to the Nam Kiu valley and Hkāmti, a route said to be the chief one used by the people trading between Hkāmti and Assam. These people are generally on the move between November and March, the rest of the year the passes are impossible either owing to heavy rainy seasons or by being blocked by snow.

Another route from Assam to Hkāmti Lông as yet untravelled by Europeans, and described only by the people, lies up the Lohit for ten days where the Ghalang river joins in, thence seven days up this, passing many Meju Mishmi villages to the Nam-kiu valley, crossing *en route* a very high and difficult range. This route is spoken of as being only open during October and November. A route from Hkāmti Lông is spoken of (also only by the people) as connecting with Thibet and running along the watershed of the Nam-kiu and Brahmaputra (Lohit branch) across the Mishmi hills. Beyond this is said to be a Thibetan fort armed with cannon which guards the pass.

Hkāmti Lông is connected with Burma by routes to the Hukong valley and Mayangkwan, and further north and east by a route leading to Sachyi on the Mali-kha, and thence down the Irrawadi to Myitkhyina. But these are only known about from native sources of information; it is known, though, that a quantity of rubber is brought down along them.

From Myitkhyina the best known routes into China are those viâ Sadōn and Simā to Tengyueh, and which are regularly used by traders, the second viâ Simā being the easiest and most resorted to.

From Bhamo run several trade routes, the chief of which are those to Tengyueh viâ Momauk, viâ Singlamkābā, viâ Lwejebūm, which are good bridle paths up to the border, and thence on become rough country tracks. A cart road is made up the Taping river from Bhamo, which eventually will be continued up to the Chinese border at Nampaung.

From Lashio in the North Shan hills, which forms

the headquarters of the frontier posts on the extreme north-east of our borderland, a good bridle path runs 120 odd miles to the further outpost on the Chinese border at Hsawn Peng, while from Lashio east a good track connects with the Kūnlôn ferry on the Salween river. This latter is also a trade route, but a very difficult one between this part of Burma and Yünnan Fu. It was at one time intended to continue the railway line from Lashio on to the Kūnlôn ferry, and possibly even further, thus to tap the trade from Southern China, but monetary considerations prevailed as well as physical difficulties against this scheme reaching fulfilment. The line was stopped at Lashio, and it was left for the French across the Mekhong to carry their railway inland from Tonquin to Yünnan Fu.

The chief means of lateral communication between Upper Assam and Upper Burma are :—

(1) From the Assam-Bengal Railway (Manipur Road Station) viâ Kohima and the Naga hills to Imphal in Manipur. A good, well-graded, metalled and bridged cart road, forty-eight miles to Kohima (the headquarters of the Naga hills district), and thence on eighty-eight miles to Imphal, the capital of the Manipur State. Good rest-houses at every stage, of which there are twelve. From Imphal on sixty-four miles of good bridle path and Tammoo, the Burma Military Police outpost in the Kale Kabaw valley, is reached, and thirty-six miles further the Chindwyn river at Sittaung, on which Flotilla steamers ply.

(2) Further south another route connects Silchar on the Assam-Bengal Railway with Imphal (Manipur) by an excellent bridle path well graded and bridged, and with small rest-houses at each of the nine stages.

(3) To the north is the Hukong valley route from Dibrugarh to Ledo, thence over the N'bon pass on the Patkoi range into the Hukong valley to Mayangkwan and thence through the Amber and Jade Mine

country to Mogoung on the Upper Burma Railway system. This has been surveyed and explored by parties from Assam and from Burma, who met at Mayangkwan, and the results of their visit proved the feasibility of the proposed railway to connect Upper Assam with Upper Burma over a length of 284 miles.

(4) An alternative route to Manipur, but which could only be traversed by small parties of troops, is that from Shillong to Juwai and Haflong, a Civil station in the North Cachar hills, and from there viâ Gueilon to the Henema outpost in the south of the Naga hills. This was in the past a good bridle path throughout, but has been almost abandoned east of Gueilon for very many years. A new alignment is, however, now being cut east from Haflong, and the disused section to Henema will probably be re-opened out. From Henema to Manipur is five long marches along roughish village tracks and through a mountainous, difficult country.

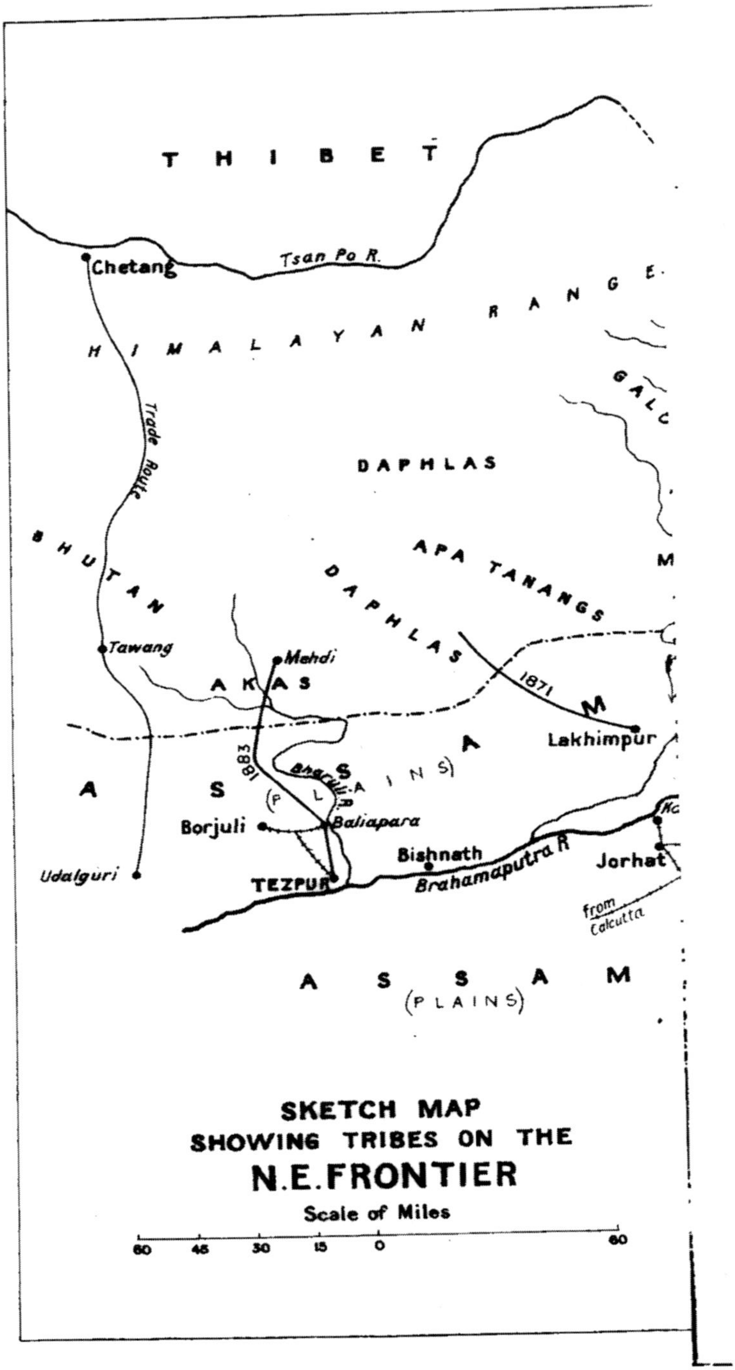

SKETCH MAP
SHOWING TRIBES ON THE
N.E.FRONTIER
Scale of Miles

INDEX

S

INDEX

C

D

H

L

N

R

S

T

R. CLAY AND SONS, LTD., BRUNSWICK ST., S.E., AND BUNGAY, SUFFOLK.